Ex   Team.

CW01511084

MANAGING SCHOOLS IN THE COMMUNITY

Managing Schools
in the
Community

Phil Street

arena

Published by
Arena
Ashgate Publishing Limited
Gower House
Croft Road
Aldershot
Hants GU11 3HR
England

Ashgate Publishing Company
Old Post Road
Brookfield
Vermont 05036
USA

British Library Cataloguing in Publication Data

Street, Phil
    Managing schools in the community
    1. Community schools   2. School management
    and administration
    I. Title
    371'.03

Library of Congress Catalog Card Number: 96-78852

ISBN 1 85742 352 6

Typeset by Raven Typesetters, Chester, and printed
in Great Britain by Hartnolls Ltd, Bodmin.

Contents

Preface

This book has taken a considerable amount of my time to prepare and write. It has drawn upon my experience of visiting schools across the country and has been informed by meetings I have held with colleagues from schools involved in their communities. I never cease to be amazed or fail to be impressed by the energy and spirit shown by colleagues who are committed to supporting and strengthening their school's work with the community. Staff at all levels contribute to ensuring that very many schools play a key role in their community. Despite the burden of various other demands and duties, and the limited supply of resources, schools continue to develop their work in the community in an enthusiastic and creative manner. It is as a consequence of this ability to 'draw blood out of a stone' that this country has developed such an outstanding record in terms of the role of schools in the community. Although not unique, few other nations have examples of the range and type of community involvement that can be found in this country's schools.

Even since I began writing this book circumstances have changed. Schools are increasingly becoming not only locations for community education, but venues for community-based learning of all kinds, including education, vocational training, health education, environmental awareness and learning about methods for combating crime. However, despite this growing range of activities, schools continue to have untapped potential as places for community-based learning.

This publication is aimed at all managers who are interested in developing the relationship between school and the community, whether they work in primary or secondary schools, local authority departments or voluntary organisations. It should assist school governors, headteachers and other senior school managers, including staff with community responsibilities, in considering the most appropriate approach to their community. Furthermore, education advisers and officers and other local authority and voluntary organisation personnel should find it useful in formulating school and community strategies.

Throughout this book readers will find a series of activities that they may wish to consider individually or use in their present or an adapted form as part of a training programme for governors, staff or other interested parties. These activities aim to encourage readers to reflect on issues contained in the various sections of the book. Their overall objective is to help the reader apply the content of the book to his or her school's own situation. Pursuing the activities will hopefully help schools access the approach to their community which they wish to take. In addition, the activities should help in determining the stage which the school has reached in this process and the most relevant strategy for future development.

Each activity carries a symbol representing how the author feels the activities can be most effectively used. However, it is entirely up to the reader whether they follow this advice. The symbols are as follows:

R   best used for personal reflection.
D   best used as the basis for discussion with appropriate colleagues, staff, governors and/or members of the community.
T   best used as part of in-service or all-school training.

Most activities carry more than one symbol, meaning that these can be used effectively in more than one way.

The activities should assist schools in their development planning and the formulation of practice.

There are a large number of people who I would like to thank for helping me write this book. Many of these are the people in schools who have, often unwittingly, provided information and insights that have helped shape its contents.

In particular, I would like to thank Anthea for her support and understanding and Paula and Christine for their tolerance and hard work in typing and revising the manuscripts.

Abbreviations

AMA	Association of Metropolitan Authorities
CA	Community Association
CEDC	Community Education Development Centre
DFEE	Department for Education and Employment
EU	European Union
ESF	European Social Fund
FE	further education
FEFC	Further Education Funding Council
FHE	Further and Higher Education Act 1992
GNVQ	General National Vocational Qualification
INSET	In-Service Education and Training
KCN	Kids Club Network
LEA	local education authority
LMS	Local Management of Schools
MBWA	Management By Walking About
NAHT	National Association of Headteachers
NIACE	National Institute for Adult and Continuing Education
NSCN	National School and Community Network
NYA	National Youth Agency
OFSTED	Office for Standards in Education
PLA	Pre-school Learning Alliance
SHA	Secondary Headteachers Association
SLA	Service Level Agreement
SRB	Single Regeneration Budget
SWOT	Strengths, Weaknesses, Opportunities and Threats
TEC	Training and Enterprise Council
WEA	Workers' Educational Association

1 Are all schools community schools?

Milestones in the development of community schooling

This book has been prepared at a time when the interest in the role of schools in their community has reached an unprecedented level. Government, opposition parties, headteacher associations and a wide range of other agencies are exploring the various contributions that schools can make to their wider community. The extent of this contribution ranges from the ability of schools to promote greater community coherence through to the value the community can add to school improvement and pupils' performance.

The community dimension of schools now encompasses a large number of issues including links with business, parental involvement, a location for vocational training for adults, provision of sports and recreation opportunities and the enrichment of the curriculum.

The conscious formulation of the school's role in its community can be traced back over 70 years to the time when Henry Morris created the community school or, more accurately, the village college. This former chief education officer for Cambridgeshire and celebrated founder of the community school movement in this country set out his original thoughts in a memorandum to members of the Cambridgeshire Education Committee just before Christmas 1923. His idea was to establish schools that provided cradle-to-the-grave education. He envisaged schools that not only provided statutory education, but were also locations for sport, recreation, cultural pursuits and adult education.

He spent much of the 1930s and 1940s turning his ideas into practice by opening a series of village colleges throughout Cambridgeshire. Apparently he was surprised that this concept did not immediately take root elsewhere. In fact, it was not until Leicestershire took up the idea in the late

1

1940s that another authority developed a planned approach to community schools.

Morris's concept of schools playing a central role in the development of their communities did not truly come of age until very recently. Only in the last 30 years has there emerged a wide-scale recognition of the importance of the school's links with home and the wider community. Indeed, the inclusion of community schools in government reports is a relatively recent phenomenon. They appeared most notably in the Plowden Report, where reference was made to their contribution to improving the quality of life in urban areas.

The wider recognition of their role meant that from the late 1960s and throughout the 1970s, the number of community schools began to expand. Policies supporting their development were produced both by rural local education authorities (LEAs), such as Devon and Somerset, and urban LEAs, such as Coventry and Walsall. The momentum behind the development of community school policies began to accelerate. The 1980s witnessed even more authorities formulating community school policies, including Cornwall, East and West Sussex, St Helens, Clwyd, Derbyshire, North Tyneside, Northumberland and North Yorkshire.

However, a fundamental change began to emerge during the latter part of the 1980s in the relationship between LEAs and schools. The twin impetus for this change lay in education legislation and reductions in local government expenditure.

Community schools had been conceived by local education authorities. In other words, they were an entirely locally inspired concept and not a central government initiative implemented by the LEA. LEAs devised the organisation and management structures for community schools, provided their funding and were the major source of professional and technical advice.

The designation as a community school was the prerogative of the LEA and was generally applied to secondary schools. This designation was usually accompanied by bestowing upon schools a selection of 'goodies', including extra staff, upgraded sports facilities and an enhanced budget to enable the provision of adult education and youth work. However, largely due to reductions in LEA budgets, designation of this kind began to disappear. LEAs no longer had the same capacity to enhance a school's resources for community purposes and, furthermore, many of them found it difficult to maintain levels of resources to existing community schools. Consequently, the opportunity for LEAs to designate more schools receded.

Although reductions in resources has had the greatest impact upon the LEAs' powers to designate community schools, education legislation has also had its effects. The introduction of Local Management of Schools has had far-reaching effects on community schools as has the gradually increasing powers of school governing bodies. One of the unseen consequences of education legislation has been that the initiative to develop community schools has begun to move away from the LEA towards the individual school. This emerging trend has had both positive and negative results. When the LEA had the ability to make available additional resources to designated schools it proved to be both an incentive and a disincentive. On the one hand, it clearly encouraged those schools which had been designated by the LEA, as they received extra resources; on the other, it discouraged many other schools from pursuing a community school approach, as defined by the LEA, because they were not in receipt of additional resources.

This is not to suggest that an interest in following a community school approach only existed in schools that were so designated. In fact, in many LEAs, schools, particularly primary schools, did develop their own strategies towards establishing a community school usually without ever being formally designated. They recognised the benefits of being a community school and so developed approaches as and when resources and opportunities permitted.

The gradual reduction in LEA budgets for community schools has raised some fundamental questions. Those schools which formerly received LEA resources have had to do some soul-searching and ask themselves whether they want to continue to be a community school and, if so, what sort of post-LEA-funded community school will they be. Those who have never received LEA resources, but have been interested in a community school approach, now find themselves on a more level playing field with the LEA-designated community schools and are beginning to examine ideas regarding the kind of community school they would like to establish.

I argue, in this book, that all schools can become community schools but that every school will face different circumstances. Each school will encounter different opportunities and different challenges. For instance, the communities which schools serve will differ enormously; some will be quite affluent while others will be extremely disadvantaged. Schools are not pre-cluded from being a community school by phase. Primary, as well as secondary, schools can develop a community approach. Nor are schools restricted by the legal status. Community schools can be maintained schools, voluntary-aided or controlled, or grant-maintained. In future community schools are more likely to be designated by their governing body – that is, if they are designated at all, since some schools will take on the role of a community school without adopting the label.

Because of these factors the term 'community school' will be used through-out the book as applying to any school involved in its community whether or not it is so designated. The term 'community school' should not distract man-agers from the perspective that being a community school is more to do with attitude than title.

Trends suggest that two principal community school models will probably emerge. The first will be those that have been designated by the LEA and, despite the loss or reduction of LEA resources, choose to remain a community school. The second will be the self-designated schools which have never received LEA resources, but are committed to a community school approach. However, in future, both types of school will face similar issues. This book aims to help schools consider the issues and formulate practical and realistic responses.

What is a community school?

Before proceeding it is important to explore further what is understood by the term 'community school'. The common conception of a community school is that of a secondary school with additional facilities for sport and recreation, an adult education programme and a youth club. It is also expected that community schools will have at least one member of staff with the title of community tutor or community coordinator. In addition to these basic characteristics, some community schools have additional specialist facilities including a community room, a bar, a fitness room and, occasionally, a swimming pool and squash courts.

The influence of this perception has meant that it is easy to see why many people equate community schools with joint use and why community education has been perceived as a bolt-on extra. There is still a widely held belief that community schools are those institutions which actively promote community use of premises. However, the definition of a community school being a location for sophisticated forms of dual use is not the one taken by this book. It is far too narrow a definition, neither reflecting the essential nature of a community school nor adequately encompassing the range of schools actively pursuing a community school approach.

Nor is the view taken at the other end of the spectrum, which insists all schools are community schools, upheld here. Those who hold this view argue that schools inevitably have a relationship with their surrounding community as no school can be an island! This interpretation is far too vague to be useful to managers. All schools can be community schools, but they cannot automatically regard themselves as such. It is argued in this book that becoming a community school has to be based upon conscious decisions taken by management and backed up by appropriate working practices and activities. The book takes the standpoint that a key determinant of a community school is its values and ethos. Evidence of the implementation of these values can be checked out by auditing the school against five operational principles that should be present in any community school. These operational principles are:

1 **access** to educational, recreational, social and cultural opportunities for the whole community;

2   the provision of **lifelong education** in a variety of forms and the development of lifelong learners;
3   the development of the **relevant curriculum** and community involvement to enhance the delivery of the National Curriculum;
4   the promotion of **interagency collaboration** and partnerships to attempt to meet the needs of their communities;
5   community involvement in the **governance** of the community school and in the provision of its activities.

Schools will interpret these five operational principles through their practice in a variety of ways which are shaped by their circumstances, including:

- location
- facilities
- type of school
- availability of resources
- the nature of the communities they serve.

The litmus test of a community school, or the extent to which a school is moving towards being a community school, is the degree to which the operational principles of community education are evident in the school's practice.

Managers of community schools, or schools interested in developing as such, should consider the concept of community schools in terms of a developmental process. History, circumstances and commitment may all contribute to the point a school has reached in that developmental process but, because of constant change, schools are unlikely to believe that they will ever reach the end of that process.

In order to ensure progress is being made towards achieving the goals of developing a community school, managers will need to concentrate on the five operational principles and the pursuit of practice that supports their realisation.

1   **Management of access.** Managers should consider how accessible their school is to the community. This will include issues of both physical and psychological access. Managers should consider everything from signposting to reception facilities, from teacher attitudes to taster courses and familiarisation activities in an effort to identify the factors which encourage and restrict access.
2   **Management of lifelong education.** Community schools should be venues for lifelong education. Different groups and individuals will have different needs. Age, ethnicity, gender, economic status and mobility will all affect an individual's ability to participate. Content, style, time and location will all influence decisions about whether an individual wishes to participate. Managers will want to consider a differentiated

programme of activities which meets a variety of interests and tastes if lifelong education is to be a feature of the school.

3   **Management of the curriculum.** The extent to which the curriculum offered by the school is relevant to the community is an important consideration for managers in community schools. Community schools will want to encourage the development of a community dimension to the National Curriculum. However, the curriculum which the school offers the community will have to be much broader than that which is taught to pupils in the classroom and will need to tackle issues of importance to people living in the community. The school will want to develop new skills, knowledge and understanding that are negotiated with, and sometimes determined by, the community.

4   **Management of interagency collaboration.** Partnership will be central to the development of the community school. Managers will want to foster and promote interagency collaboration. This will require managers to identify opportunities for collaboration, build networks with other agencies, share decision-making and encourage others to recognise the benefits of cooperation.

5   **Management of governance.** A community school manager will have to examine the degree to which the community is involved in the governance of the school. A community school gains legitimacy for its programme and activities from community consent and approval. Managers will need to give thought to creating structures for community involvement in governance and to adopting procedures for ensuring effective decisions are taken. A variety of models of governance are available to schools and these are discussed later in the book; however, developing appropriate practice and management style is more difficult to exemplify and depends heavily on the nature of the individual manager.

Activity 1.1   The five operational principles (R, D, T)

To what extent can evidence currently be found of the school's commitment to the five operational principles of community education?

1   To what extent does your school extend access to educational, recreational, social or cultural activities to the wider community? List provision and activities.

2   Are you offering lifelong educational opportunities? List provision and activities.

3   Is the community being involved and used in the delivery of the National Curriculum? List examples of involvement.

4   Which other agencies is your school collaborating with to meet community needs? List agencies and purpose for collaboration.
5   What are the opportunities for the community to be involved in the governance or management of community school activities?

Several models of community school can currently be found. These include:

- **Use of premises model.** In this model the school facilities are used by the community for a range of activities including sport, adult education and youth work. The school has little direct involvement in the organisation or determination of the programme or events and largely acts as the landlord.
- **Joint-use model.** This usually suggests that the school or the LEA on its behalf has entered into a formal agreement with another agency to make use of its facilities. The most common form of joint use is where the local authority leisure services department or district council makes use of the school's sports facilities outside the school day. Many joint-use agreements require little or no direct active involvement by the school in the management or delivery of provision.
- **School-managed use of premises model.** This generally suggests that the school is rather more than a landlord in that it might have determined the community which it serves and might be involved in discussions with the LEA about the content of the community education programme. In some cases the school actually assumes responsibility for the management of the delivery of the community education programme. The school which pursues a community use model may have on its establishment a community education coordinator or tutor who directly manages lettings, use of sports facilities, the adult education and youth work. The school may also be involved in promoting the use of the school and be an active partner in management. In some cases, the school manages and administers the sports facilities, the use of premises by outside agencies and is responsible for the financial aspects of community education
- **Integrated community school model.** This suggests that the school is attempting to integrate the community dimension into all its aspects. In the integrated community school there would be evidence of community in the curriculum, the use of premises, the school development plan and the management structure. The community would permeate all aspects of school life and would be a key component of school policy. The school's values would contain reference to community education and many of the school's working practices would contain a community element.

Activity 1.2   A question of identity (R, D)

A school management needs to consider the model that best reflects its current situation:

What kind of community school are we?

- LEA-designated?
- Self-designated?
- Not designated but interested in developing a community school approach?

What are the benefits of being a community school?

There is no statutory requirement for a school to be a community school. Therefore, given the expectations being placed upon schools by central government it would be understandable if schools were not taking up the option of becoming a community school. However, despite the pressures, an increasing number of schools are becoming community schools. This seems to be a genuinely popular strategy, mainly because schools are recognising the benefits of adopting this approach. The major benefits can be summarised as the five 'Ps': Performance, Perception, Premises, Partnership and Participation.

Performance

Schools are subject to increased levels of monitoring and performance review. Legislation has led to the establishment of the Office for Standards in Education (OFSTED) which ensures a regular cycle of school inspections. Furthermore, schools are required to publish examination results and their test performances are publicly tabulated. The factors influencing how children learn and, therefore, their level of performance are many and various. Some are well beyond the control of the school. Research has revealed that a significant influence on the child's ability to learn is his or her parents' attitude to education and, to a lesser extent, the attitude of his or her immediate community. Children whose parents possess a positive attitude to school and demonstrate an interest in their education generally perform better than those children whose parents are disinterested. Community schools see parents as an important element of the community. Primary community schools in particular regard parents as their core community, and many have introduced ways of encouraging parental involvement in the life of the school and the education of their children.

Parental involvement in secondary school has to assume a different form. Encouraging parents to take a positive attitude to their daughters' or sons' education has to be achieved through less direct involvement. Good, clear and regular communication is the essence of parent involvement in secondary schools. Parents need to be kept informed of curriculum developments, pupil performance and other features of school life. They need to feel that the school is sensitive and responsive. A parent's impression of schools is likely to be heavily influenced by their own experience which, for too many, was typified by failure, unpleasant memories and even humiliation. Schools should look at ways of counteracting any negative feelings parents might have by developing constructive and meaningful relationships.

Perception

The advent of market forces in public sector education has been one of the factors that has led schools to become more conscious of their public image. In particular, they have aimed to avoid rumour or disinformation circulating about the school. Community schools have built-in advantages in this area. Their accessibility has enabled parents and other members of the community to form their own opinions and judgements about the school. Moreover they are characterised by a regular flow of communication and information to the community through newsletters, news releases and circulars. Community schools represent open systems; they are 'community-friendly' and describe themselves as welcoming and approachable. They attempt to create the right atmosphere for actively listening to parents and the community and taking their views seriously. Community schools base their provision on expressed and visible need and deploy various strategies to assess that need. The most effective strategy is by sustaining a two-way communication of both a formal and informal kind. The necessity to engage in continuous communication maximises the possibility of the school projecting a positive image of itself and obtaining feedback from the community on its perceived performance.

Premises

The danger of placing too much emphasis upon use of premises is that it is possible to fall into the trap of assuming that community schools equals community use of facilities. Furthermore, schools – especially primary schools – which lack extensive and specialist facilities perceive themselves as disqualified from becoming a community school simply for that reason. In reality, schools which do not have specialist facilities to hire or let can be community schools. However, specialist or purpose-built community facilities can make a valuable contribution to the quality of life and the widening of recreational opportunities to the local community. Undoubtedly, community facilities are an advantage to a school which is, or wants to be, a community school but possession of enhanced premises does not automatically qualify a school as a community school.

Nevertheless, pursuing a community school approach generally does entail schools opening their facilities for community use. Many schools have spaces, ranging from sports halls to standard classrooms, within their premises which the community are interested in using. Schools with surplus accommodation have sometimes converted some of this into parents' rooms, community lounges, fitness suites, bars and accommodation for childcare.

A community school can gain enormous benefits from the use of its premises. It can:

- provide a source of income for the school
- contribute to opportunities for sport and leisure which in turn can enhance the school's image in the community
- provide a venue for meetings and celebratory events, and assist in making the school the focal point of the community
- offer a location where school staff and the community can meet on an informal, as well as formal, basis.

School premises are a resource provided as a result of community investment; they should be made available to the wider community. Schools should not be left empty and unused for long periods of time. They ought to be used during evenings, weekends and holidays if the community is to maximise the return from its investment. A further advantage of community use of premises is the effect it can have upon deterring vandals. Schools used extensively by their community often report lower levels of vandalism than schools that are not used. The school with its lights on and occupied is a less attractive target for the vandal than the unoccupied school abandoned at the end of the school day.

Partnership

There are certain things that schools cannot achieve on their own. To meet some needs schools have to enter partnerships with other people or organisations. This is true when schools attempt to meet the requirements of their pupils, but it becomes even more pressing when schools wish to respond to the wider community's needs. The type of partnerships entered into by community schools depends upon what the school is trying to achieve. Partnerships have been formed with industry to provide pupils with contact with the world of work. Similarly schools have looked for overseas partners to enable international exchange. Establishing partnerships at community level is a recognition that every community contains a richness of human and physical resources which can be harnessed to effectively meet the needs of communities.

Partnerships lead to the pooling of knowledge, skills and resources that produce an outcome which is more than the sum of the individual partners. They can rationalise the use of resources and may result in outcomes which organisations could not have achieved alone. They can spark new ideas or innovatory ways of doing things.

Partnerships can be formed with people or organisations from the community for the purpose of providing such benefits as:

- childcare
- activities for young people
- adult education
- team game experience for pupils
- cultural opportunities
- leisure facilities
- vocational training for women
- playschemes
- activities for the elderly
- citizens' advice
- healthcare.

Community schools can be the facilitating or enabling partner by providing accommodation or specialist facilities to people or organisations wishing to make provision for the community. They can also be the pro-active partner which identifies a need and establishes a partnership with a person or organisation to meet that need.

Activity 1.3 Partnership (R, T)

1 List the organisations with whom your school is currently working in partnership.
2 List the benefits and disadvantages of those partnerships.

Participation

The notion of participation conjures up a number of images. It can be understood as a word which conveys a particular style of management, or it can be used in connection with empowerment or entitlement. Regardless of how it is interpreted, its application infers *involvement*. It is involvement that gives community schools their legitimacy. However, the concept of participation in relation to community school works in two ways. Community schools should participate in the life of their community as well as the community participate in life of the school.

Community schools provide opportunities for both formal and informal community participation in management. Some community schools formalise participation through establishing community associations or community councils whose management committee members are drawn from the community. Others enable participation through user committees, forums or consultative groups.

However, a community school's commitment to participation often goes beyond management structures. Community schools attempt to create environments which foster participation in a variety of shapes and forms. For example, staff are often encouraged to assume a working style that promotes and welcomes participation: they encourage the giving of advice, they consult over decisions and consult before policy is finalised. A participatory style of leadership is highly appropriate to the community school context as it promotes a management culture which encourages involvement in decision-making with or without the existence of formal structures. This allows the schools to seize opportunities and maximise its responsiveness. Participation is a highly beneficial management style in a community school as it promotes a sense of 'ownership' of the school and encourages the exercise of initiative. It gives the opportunity to take responsibility amongst members of the community. In short, the community school values the community's greatest resource – its people.

Activity 1.4   Participation and community school management (R, D)

This activity is aimed at encouraging managers and others in schools to consider the opportunities of developing community participation in management.

1   Participation is good because it:

- encourages the taking of responsibility   True/False
- promotes ownership amongst members
  of the community   True/False
- helps to make use of members of the
  community's skills and talents.   True/False

2   List what you see as:
   a)   the advantages of participation
   b)   the challenges of participation.

---

2 Going community

How does a school become a community school?

Many of the schools that are currently designated as community schools will already know that, in the not too dim and distant past, schools could only assume the designation of community school when approval was given by the LEA. Indeed, in some authorities it remains the accepted tradition that only the LEA possesses the right to designate and, in these areas, schools are discouraged from adopting the label if the LEA has not given their consent.

It seems unlikely that such an attitude can be sustained for much longer. The extension of local management powers and changes in LEA roles is inevitably leading to an acknowledgement that the initiation and continuation of a community school is becoming the responsibility of the headteacher and governing body. The LEA will remain a significant partner, but their relationship to community schools will continue to change. Furthermore, there are indications that designation is not a significant issue since some schools are deciding to practise a community school approach, but are not bothering to incorporate the word 'community' into their titles.

In all schools that wish to develop as a community school, with or without the label, someone has to initiate the idea. The more senior the initiator the better is the chance of the idea turning into practice. Someone will need to have a vision and motivation for developing a community school approach. He or she will need to have some distinctive and powerful ideas about the shape and form the community school will take, and these ideas will have to be committed to paper.

The ideal initiator is the headteacher, although other influential senior staff may also be in a strong position to float the idea and persuade others, sometimes including the headteacher, of the advantages of assuming a community school approach. Experience proves, however, that those schools without

13

the support of the headteacher can encounter organisational problems and obstacles to the development of a community school.

The initiator needs to share his or her ideas with other senior staff and obtain their opinions on the best approach to 'going community'. Early indication of the interest in developing a community school approach ought to be given to the governing body and its members should be given explanations as to the implications of this course of action.

Values or mission

Once the idea has been broached the next step is to consider the purpose of the community school. There is no universal definition of what is a community school. Each school has to respond to its community and, because no two communities are exactly the same, each school's approach will have to be different.

However, although community schools are not precisely the same there are some commonalities. All community schools do share a commitment to a wider community beyond that of the pupils of statutory school age and reflect this commitment through a variety of activities, programmes and services. This commitment is always underpinned by the belief that education is a lifelong process and that schools have an integral role to fulfil in their community. Although this belief may already be held by a wide range of staff within the school, far too often it has neither been written down nor codified.

Prompted by modern management theorists, schools have begun to introduce value or mission statements. This is an essential prerequisite for a community school. Why? Because the success of a community school rests on its ethos and this is based upon its values. Of course, schools have always had values; they are the guiding nostrums that indicate what a school gives worth to or regards as important. These values, written, or unwritten, are generally understood if not always shared by the whole staff and governors. A school's values influence the bestowing of rewards and the imposing of sanctions.

Values are not external, nor are they to be confused with aims. Aims form a target on a distant horizon which all strive to eventually reach. People *live* values. They affect their attitudes, their demeanour and their approach. They inform the way people work and influence the establishment of priorities and the allocation of resources.

The values of a community school must articulate the school's commitment to its community. They will be broad statements, but they will tell staff, pupils, governors and the wider community about the kind of school they work in, send their children to or use.

Drawing up a value statement

The process of preparing a value statement is not a task to be completed and then ticked off on a 'jobs to do' list. A statement of values takes time to formulate, introduce and embed into a school. Values have to become virtually a habit. They have to be lived out and must inform patterns of behaviour and working practices.

The stages detailed below are nothing more than a critical path to the establishment of a value statement: the development of a meaningful value statement must be a continuous process which is never genuinely completed.

Stage one

- Senior management draws up a draft value statement.
- Senior management consults governors and invites their ideas and involvement.
- The school consults staff through a questionnaire or personal interviews.
- The school consults parents and community and invites responses.

Stage two

- Senior management plans an INSET day to help to identify, and provide an opportunity to discuss, the school's values.
- The in-service day should attempt to include all school staff, non-teaching staff, governors and personnel from agencies with which the school has regular contact.

An idea for the content of an INSET day is shown in the following example.

Community Education and Schools In-Service Training Day

Programme

Session one: What is a community school?
Discussion and activities.

Session two: Who is our community?
Activity to identify the school's community.

Session three: What is our school doing in the community?
Activities to carry out an audit of the curriculum and other areas community involvement and contact.

Session four: How does the community see our school?
Activity to try to examine how members of the community see the school and become involved in the school.

Session five: What does our community need?
Activity to try to estimate or assess community needs.

Session six: Why should the school be involved in the community?
Activity to identify the benefits and challenges from being involved in the community.

Session seven: What can the school do to be more involved in the community?
Activity designed to ask the school to explore what the school can realistically do in the community it serves.

Session eight: What is the next step?
Activity to focus action – what, who, when and how?

Stage three

- Staff/governors review and identify values and practical impact of their adoption.
- Senior management consult governors.
- Senior management prepare statement of values and:

    - present to the governors, with a copy for each person
    - present to all staff at a staff meeting, with copy for each person
    - circulate to the community.

A number of schools have pursued the process described above, and the example below sets out a community school's value statement.

Value statement developed by Queen's Park High School in Chester

Policy statement: community education

Rationale
The school exists within a rich and varied social, cultural and economic context. Community education is about bringing the life of the school and the life of the communities it serves into a close and mutually rewarding relationship. As such, it should be developed as an integral part of a whole school approach to teaching and learning, enriching the

educational experience of all students and thus raising standards of achievement.

Community education is a commitment which underpins and permeates all aspects of the life and work of the school. As such, it should inform all staff development activity and be subject to continuous review and evaluation.

Purposes

- To encourage community access to the physical resources and professional expertise of the school.
- To develop the school's use of the community as a resource for curriculum development and education for citizenship and for the world of work.
- To enhance the quality of relationships between all members of the school community.
- To promote effective communication and closer partnership between home and school, teachers and parents.
- To raise the profile of the school within the local area and develop people's confidence in it.

Activity 2.1   Values and the school in the community (R, D, T)

Consider the following question:

Does community education affect our school values?

This activity is designed to assist and support further reflection on the identification and introduction of values that are realisable and have the potential for being operated in school.

A common feature of many schools in the past was the school motto, generally in Latin, which appeared on school badges. Few modern organisations have mottos but an increasing number have value statements. An organisation's value statement sets out what the organisation believes in – what it considers worthwhile and important. It is aimed at influencing the way people behave and what they do. It tells everybody what to expect of the organisation.

A community education approach must be taken into account when a school begins to draw up its value statement. Below is a selection of statements which have appeared in various organisations' value statements. Choose five that might appeal to schools interested in furthering the community dimension and rank them 1–5 in order of importance.

Consider on your own, or discuss with other staff and governors the statements chosen and their order of importance.

1   We are committed to meeting the educational needs of all students.
2   We will provide educational, sporting, recreational and social opportunities to all without distinction or prejudice.
3   We value all people equally.
4   We will prepare people for citizenship in a democracy through working interactively with the local, and wider, community.
5   We will encourage autonomy and experimentation along with perseverance.
6   We support partnership and participation in management.
7   We will aim for the highest standard of educational provision.
8   We will be best in everything we do.
9   We will provide excellent educational opportunities for the whole community.
10   We will promote working partnerships between students, parents and staff.

Formulating values

The formulation, or writing, of values is inevitably a time consuming process if it is to be carried out effectively, mainly because values have to be 'owned' by the school, its staff and its management. The task cannot be delegated to an individual or a group and presented for approval to the whole school staff. Certainly someone has to write an initial draft, but those who do so must be prepared to accept revision, amendment and even rewriting. They must perceive their role as initiators of the process. Preparing a values statement involves considerable work.

Two things should be kept in mind: first, the values must encapsulate the school's community educational purpose; second, they must be capable of being put into practice. Figure 2.1 suggests how a school may wish to go about introducing a value statement.

There will be members of staff who will strongly welcome the development of a value statement that supports the concept of a community school. However, others will find it difficult to accept every part of the value statement and, in a small number of cases, to any part of the statement. Management will need to be prepared for this eventuality, although those who cannot identify with the values or be persuaded of the benefits will be expected not to be obstructive. In order to limit any sense of antipathy among sections of the school staff towards the development of a community school every effort should be made to involve the majority of the staff in the preparation of a value statement. Preparing a school's community education value statement should not be seen as an exclusive process involving only the chosen few. By involving the widest number of people in negotiating the school's

Figure 2.1 Drawing up a value statement

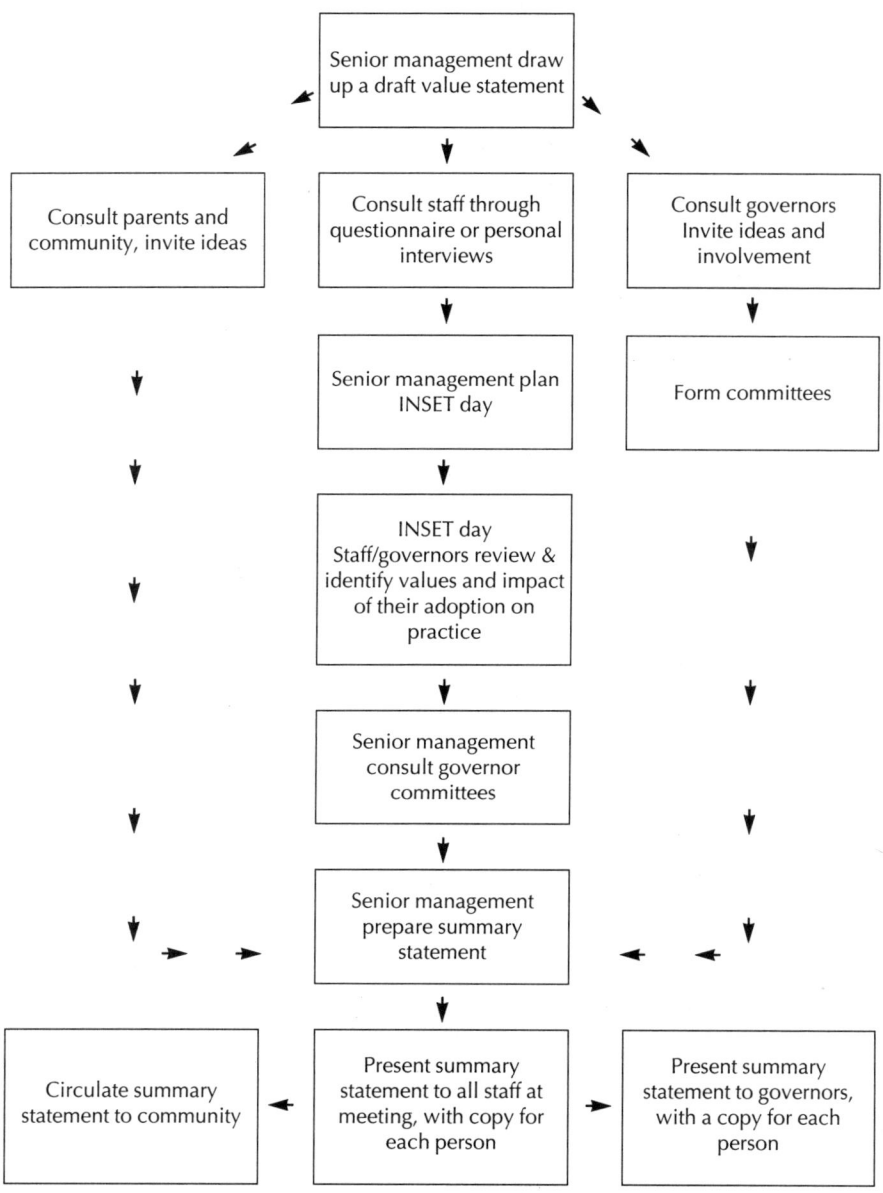

Source: Street (1992).

values, ownership will be dispersed throughout the school and the likelihood of alienating large sections of the school staff will be avoided. In developing a clear statement of values the school is telling all, both currently and in the future, what they stand for and to what they give value.

The role of leadership in community schools

The concept of the integrated community school, in which the whole school has assumed responsibility for the policy, provision and management of community education, was raised in Chapter 1 (page 7). In this model community education is part of the school's weft and weave. The headteacher and the school governing body are crucial to the development of an integrated approach. The headteacher assumes a particularly central role because through his or her actions, decisions and behaviour he or she indicates the importance of community education in the school. This leadership role may encompass being the initiator of the concept in the school, it may be to actively support the efforts of champions within the school, or it could include encouraging policies and priorities which create greater involvement with the wider community. In the book *In Search of Excellence* (Peters and Waterman, 1982) Tom Peters talks of transforming leadership. This is a style of leadership that does not wish to retain power over all decisions and actions. Transforming leadership, Peters says, celebrates the creation of other leaders. It is a leadership that fosters initiative and welcomes innovation. This style of leadership is highly suitable for community schools in that it accepts participation in decision-making and recognises that many may wish to contribute to the development of its activities.

Champions

It may be useful at this stage to introduce the concept of the champion. According to Tom Peters and Robert Waterman (1982), successful innovations often revolve around the fired-up champion. Champions should be encouraged to come forward, grow and flourish. Peters and Waterman talk of the champion as being 'possessed by the idea'. They believe in the need for the volunteer champion, and this concept can be usefully employed in furthering the kinds of development associated with nearly all aspects of community education. To school managers who want to introduce an innovation, the champion can be an enormous asset in terms, for instance, of working with human resources and developing appropriate attitudes and approaches. In the early years of a community school the champion might be a member of the teaching staff who is enthusiastic and willing to encourage parents into the classroom. This kind of champion can offer an important role model.

If the innovation is successful, he or she may encourage others to pursue similar approaches.

The leadership skills required in community schools are multifaceted. The leadership will find that it has to advocate for all, negotiate between parties where interests and needs collide and possess an understanding of the various dimensions that exist within the community education programme.

In community schools, the leadership will need to embrace a wide range of activities and understand the principles which inform their practice. For example, the leadership will have to become acquainted with the principles that underpin youth work, as this has many differences from that of the mainstream school in its approach to education.

Developing the ethos of the community school

Over the years some have commented that community education is easier to define as a set of beliefs than as a practice. Certainly, beliefs are important in establishing an appropriate ethos for community education in schools. As already stated, these beliefs should be encapsulated in the school's values statement, but they should be operationalised through management decisions and the day-to-day life of the school.

A fundamental influence upon the way the values are interpreted is the attitude of management. It will form a crucial role model in the generation of an appropriate ethos.

In his book, *Writing Home*, Alan Bennett describes in one chapter entitled 'Dinner at Noon' his childhood recollections of a visit to a Harrogate hotel. For many years nowhere filled him with the same unease as did a hotel. They were places where people had to be on their best behaviour, and when this happens people are not always at their best. He refers to hotels as having been 'theatres of humiliation' but goes on to compliment the modern hotel industry on the changes that have been brought about in seeming to have created an environment that is comfortable, relaxed and straightforward. According to Bennett's observations, hotels are not intimidating establishments, in fact he could almost be saying that modern hotels are very much user-friendly organisations. Community schools also need to be user- or community-friendly. Some of our schools remain distant and forbidding places which some members of the community associate with unpleasant memories and failure. These days, community schools are actively promoting a more positive ethos through a number of strategies, including the attitude of reception staff, the provision of social facilities and through the manner adopted by the teaching staff. The leadership should encourage and reinforce this ethos, ensuring that visitors and community members, so long as they conform to appropriate requirements, are treated with respect and decency.

This community-friendly ethos takes time to develop and become ingrained. It will require in-service training, discussions and, above all, appropriate role models being set by management. Most school staff, both teaching and non-teaching, are positive in their relations with the wider community, but their attitude will be strengthened when they see senior management advocating and pursuing a similar style.

Activity 2.2   Schools and governors (R, T)

Is developing community schooling going to hurt?

This activity has been prepared as an aid in the difficult process of turning values into action.

Value statements are useless if they are not put into practice, but may mean that people have to change their attitudes and the way they do things. Because people like stability and doing familiar things, change rarely occurs without some pain. Change means challenging the accepted way of behaving and introducing new routines and approaches.

Adopting a set of community education values should have a perceptible effect on what happens within a school. In Activity 2.1 (page 17–18) it was suggested that five value statements might be selected. The list below contains evidence of how 'living out' the values might be demonstrated. Underline the features that might be seen in a school which has adopted community education values so that you can visualise future practice and its implications.

- parents assisting in the classroom
- friendly and pleasant receptionist
- comfortably furnished reception area with magazines
- clear hiring arrangements
- adults learning in school
- polite approach to members of the community
- accessible appointment system for parents to meet school staff
- educational guidance for adults available
- community involved in the curriculum
- participation encouraged by school management
- regular assessment of community needs
- members of the community seen in the school

Different approaches in primary and secondary schools

There is a widely held opinion among many of those involved in community education that primary schools are the most natural kind of community schools. They are generally closer to their communities and parents, in particular, feel that primary schools are approachable and friendly. There are several factors mitigating in favour of primary schools. These advantages include their smaller size, and therefore less forbidding buildings, their daily contact with parents when they bring their children to school and the parents' generally higher motivation to support their children's education when their children are younger. Although not all primary schools have seen their work with parents as community education, in fact many primary schools have been practising community education for years, but often without realising it.

This concentration on involving parents takes place in a variety of forms, including:

- home visiting
- links with preschool provision
- parents in the classroom
- parents and pupil visits
- parent groups
- parental involvement in their children's learning
- parent and toddler groups.

Many primary schools also make their premises available to various clubs and organisations, but their main focus is work with parents.

In this country there are a number of purpose-built community primary schools which have facilities over and above those normally found in such schools. In addition to these purpose-built community primary schools, some primary schools have been either LEA- or self-designated as community schools. This designation has sometimes been a consequence of the availability of spare capacity which has enabled schools to dedicate areas within their buildings for community activities.

The combination of schools that are naturally close to their communities with the provision of extra facilities can be a highly successful formula, as demonstrated by a variety of primary schools. Through sensitive and careful management these schools have built up extensive community education programmes. However, as many primary schools have demonstrated, they do not have to possess additional facilities to undertake effective community education nor do they have to be LEA- or self-designated.

In secondary schools the main focus for management is often on programme provision. This is not to suggest that work with parents is not regarded as important. However, the central preoccupation is with the organisation and delivery of activities. The simple fact that secondary schools have facilities which the community wants to use naturally guides the direction of management. Effective and efficient use of premises requires time and energy to organise. Secondary schools are also often used as locations for both vocational and non-vocational adult education programmes. The degree of involvement which secondary school management may have in adult education will vary according to local circumstances, but in certain cases secondary school management assumes a considerable level of responsibility for programming, budget and administration. Secondary schools are occasionally centres for youth work and this may carry with it direct or indirect management responsibilities.

Another external factor influencing the role of secondary school managers are the expectations of the business community, who appear to welcome more sophisticated and complex links with secondary schools compared with those expected of primary schools. Furthermore, it is generally anticipated that secondary schools will involve students, and occasionally staff, in providing community service and outreach activities.

Scale has a major impact upon the difference between managing a community primary school and a community secondary school. Usually, secondary schools have larger premises, are open for longer periods of time and have greater levels of community use. Primary schools do have community use, but this occupies a small amount of management's time which is more often directed towards work with parents and families.

The fundamental skills required to manage a community primary or secondary school are similar; the differences are more to do with the types of activities and the clientele they address, than about the philosophy and practice of management. Management in primary schools tends to concentrate on work with parents, while in secondary schools it is on facility management and work with the wider community.

Activity 2.3   Differences between primary and secondary schools in the community (R)

It may prove useful to reflect on the differences that managers of primary community schools and secondary community schools encounter. In order to do this,

1   List the differences that could be expected between primary and secondary schools involved in their community.
2   Consider what are the principle implications for managers as a consequence of these differences.

Through identifying the management similarities and differences, the significant issues affecting the role of headteachers in primary and secondary community schools will probably be clarified.

Developing participation in community school management

Community education is not done *to* people, but is done *with* people, community participation is therefore a key indicator that this is being achieved. Community participation in management contributes towards legitimising the community school. Unfortunately, it is more easily said than done! Its effectiveness depends upon it

- providing a broad and balanced perspective from the community rather than a narrow set of opinions
- having an organisational structure through which the community's views can be articulated
- achieving broad consensus and minimising unnecessary conflict.

Although managers recognise the benefits of community participation they sometimes lack experience and confidence in its operation. Uncertainty and the fear of the unknown sometimes account for the existence of a cautious attitude among community school managers towards community participation. However, few, if any, community schools do not have mechanisms for community participation, the most common form of which is what Tom Peters calls 'active listening'. Headteachers and designated community education staff dedicate many hours to obtaining opinions, ideas and perceptions from members of the community. Of course, in some schools their community programmes are still based upon the professional 'hunch', but even this hunch is most likely informed by discussions with the community. For instance, it is not unknown for community education meetings in community schools to appear to attract only limited contributions from members of the community. At first sight, it seems that community representatives at the meeting say nothing. Evidence suggests, however, that when community representatives are quizzed about the style of meetings and asked if they are happy for the headteacher and community staff to do most of the talking, they often accept that it is entirely appropriate to conduct meetings in this way so long as the community staff are available and involved in 'active listening' outside these meetings. This pursuit of 'active listening' ensures that the meetings reflect a cross-section of community opinions.

Management's role, it seems, is to create the environment for community participation to take place, but its form and structure will have to be left to individuals and the schools to determine.

There are a variety of models of community school management systems. In the past LEAs determined the management structure which community schools operated. LEA designation brought not only additional staff and extra funding, but also a requirement to establish a management system laid down by the LEA. The changing role of the LEA has meant that self-designated community schools are no longer required to establish authority-approved management systems, although, in fact, many schools are influenced by those systems existing in LEA-inspired community schools.

There are a number of models and variants of management systems. An attempt has been made here to categorise the different management systems into four main types: the community association model, the community council model, the user committee model and the governor subcommittee model.

The community association model

In this model an independent Community Association (CA) has been established and is based on the school. The CA is often a registered charity with an approved Charity Commission constitution. It becomes responsible for the community education programme, and the headteacher is often a member of its management committee. It is common practice for the member of school staff with responsibility for the community to act as the executive officer for the CA. The best known example of this was the approach found in Walsall. There, the LEA contracted with the CA to provide a community education programme and delegated a budget to the CA to support its implementation. Other local authorities have also established a community association model, but few have set these up as independent registered charities.

This approach has both benefits and disadvantages. Its benefits are that:

- it ensures genuine community participation
- it provides an opportunity for making funding applications to a wide variety of organisations
- it shares responsibility for provision.

Its disadvantages include the following:

- it can reinforce a bolt-on or non-integrated approach
- it can lead to the growth of diverse and conflicting interests between school and the CA
- it can lead to the school absolving itself of responsibility for community education
- it possibly creates opportunities for a narrow and sometimes unrepresentative group to dominate decision-making.

Community council model

A number of LEAs have introduced the community council model. One of the conditions of LEA designation as a community school is that the school agrees to establish a community council. The LEA usually issues guidelines on type and form of the constitution and operational activities of these councils. Usually they have representation from:

- governors
- school management
- non-teaching staff
- users of the community activities
- special interests – that is, ethnic minorities
- the youth service.

In many cases, the community council enters into an arrangement with the authority for the delivery of services and, through a Service Level Agreement, targets and outcomes are established and agreed. The remit of the community council is sometimes extended beyond the school so that it assumes responsibility for an area or 'patch' adjacent to the school. The community council membership is extended to take account of this and, consequently, the Service Level Agreement includes reference to provision beyond the school. The advantages of this model are that:

- it provides the opportunity for community participation
- it offers a forum to discuss policy and user requirements
- it creates a system of accountability.

The disadvantages include the following:

- it may become a 'rubber-stamping' group for school management decisions
- it may not represent the wider community's interest, but only those of current users
- it requires time and energy to service and support the council's work.

Rochdale, Derbyshire and Cambridgeshire are among those LEAs that have established community councils.

User committee model

User committees are usually established by the school to receive feedback and views on such issues as the facilities, letting arrangements, programme range and customer satisfaction. The precise role of these committees vary, as some are consultative bodies that are convened perhaps twice a year while others have a more direct and substantial influence on policy, programme and direction. The user committees, as would be expected, comprise representatives of users of the school and include:

- senior management
- adult education staff
- youth work staff
- representatives of groups and clubs making use of the school premises
- representatives of the adult students.

Because these committees generally do not have any non-user representation, issues consequently focus on the ideas, needs and concerns of current users and rarely consider matters of wider community interest. The advantages of this model are as follows:

- it provides a forum for users
- it offers the opportunity to assess user satisfaction
- it can be the source of ideas or a sounding-board for developments.

The disadvantages include the following:

- the committee has a limited role and is therefore often poorly attended
- it cannot effectively represent the community
- it can become a forum for people to represent the narrow interests of their clubs, class or group.

Governor subcommittee model

The Education (No. 2) Act 1986 did not permit delegation of control of premises by the school governors to other organisations. Consequently, the school governors had to remain in control of school premises at all times. This meant that, unless action had been taken to formally transfer control of premises from the school, many of the dual-use arrangements became null and void and governors lost the ability to delegate the use of premises to community councils and associations.

The government recognised that this had been a piece of ill-thought-out legislation and agreed to amend it as soon as an appropriate opportunity arose. In the meantime they issued a directive that school governors could establish subcommittees which could include non-governors, but in which only members of the school governors could have voting rights.

The situation was eventually revised through the Education Act 1993 which permitted school governors, if they so chose, to enter into a transfer of control agreement with persons or organisations for the purpose of promoting community use.

Nevertheless, despite the change in legislation, many schools have retained their community education governor subcommittee. Its advantages are that:

- governors are kept informed about community education
- governors identify community education as one of their responsibilities and, therefore, they maintain a sense of ownership
- it allows for liaison regarding arrangements between the mainstream school and its community dimension.

Its disadvantages are that:

- it can be seen as the major decision-making forum, thereby excluding community participation
- there may be overemphasis upon school needs as opposed to those of the community
- it may become preoccupied with administrative matters and neglect debate about ideas, needs and concerns.

The role of school governors

Schools are assuming an increasingly important role in sustaining, promoting and developing community education. School management is filling some of the roles being vacated by LEAs in terms of making community education policy and encouraging innovation. They cannot fulfil these roles properly unless they have the support and commitment of the school's governors. The governors will need to be aware of:

- what community education means in their school
- what the implications are for them as school governors
- the content of the school's community education programme
- management and financial arrangements for community education
- any development plans, policies or personnel issues.

Some governors will particularly want to take an active role in community education to be members of a community subcommittee or community council. However, essentially all governors will need to be kept informed of developments and encouraged to recognise that community education is an integral aspect of the school that has benefits for both the pupils and the school as a whole.

Activity 2.4   Managing community schools (R)

This activity aims to encourage a general review of the key issues raised in this chapter. It consists of asking the following questions:

1   Who actually decides whether a school is to be a community school?
2   Who needs to be involved, and how, in the development of a community school?
3   What is understood by community education values?
4   What are the key roles, if any, of the following in a community school:

   – Governors?
   – Headteacher?
   – Senior management?
   – Day school staff?
   – School secretarial staff?

5   What are the advantages and disadvantages of developing structures for community participation in managing a community school?

3 Planning for action

Whom do we serve?

There is a temptation for community schools to try to be all things to everyone. The very title 'community school' seems to suggest a school that is all-inclusive and could feel that it is not achieving all its targets if one sector of the community is neglected or left out. This is, of course, setting an impossible task. However, the problem that many schools face is deciding which sectors of the community they should be aiming to serve. Commitment to the ideal that the school belongs to all of us can create a dilemma for management. Perhaps the first matter that management needs to address, as part of the process of defining who should be served, is the identification of the boundaries of its community.

Possibly the most obvious influence upon determining a school's community is its pupil catchment area. Most schools would probably accept that the catchment area forms its most easily recognisable community, or as many community organisations call the geographical community they serve, their 'area of benefit'.

In the case of those schools which have developed a management structure based on a community association their constitution will require them to determine their 'area of benefit' – that is, the geographical area to be served by the community association. This area of benefit then becomes the principal focus for the activities of the school-based community association.

Where schools have large widespread pupil catchment areas – as particularly is the case with rural secondary schools – they may see their catchment area as forming their greater community, but recognise the more immediate villages and habitats as the main focus of their activities.

Denominational community schools find that there are other dimensions which have to be considered when agreeing their communities, especially as many of these schools will attract pupils from an extremely dispersed area.

These schools will probably see a key role in serving the needs of those within the community who share their faith.

Consequently, denominational schools and also rural schools will both experience having an immediate and a more distant community to serve. Management needs to be clear about who is its community, and schools need to consider whether they wish to delineate an area of benefit. This could be done by defining a geographical 'patch', adopting the school pupil catchment area, or by recognising ward, town, district council or even traditional neighbourhood boundaries.

**Activity 3.1   Identifying the community served by
the school (R, D, T)**

School management may wish to consider whether it is necessary to define the school's community for the purposes of focusing its activities. If so, among the questions that need to be addressed will be:

- Is the school's community already defined for management?
- Which factors should management take into account in determining your school's main focus for activities?

It may help to take a look at a large-scale map of the local area. Are there any natural boundaries or major communication routes that form an artificial boundary?

It may be useful to take time to consider the issues involved in defining your community and specifying an area of benefit or main focus for activities and the problems that might arise from specifying your community.

Communities within communities

The word 'community' can be ambiguous and sometimes its application can be confusing. Generally community refers to shared interests, cultures or defined areas where people live. Some groups have a strong sense of community. They communicate regularly, share events and activities, share a common language or sense of meaning, spend time together in common pursuit and celebrate arrivals and departures together. However, for many communities the linkages holding them together are fragile. People may feel as though they merely happen to live in a certain area. They will have limited communication, even with their neighbours. They take part in few collective activities and may only be drawn temporarily together in the case of shared adversity.

Within geographical communities there are other communities – those communities of gender, of hobbies and interests, of ramblers, of football fans, of ethnic minorities, of cyclists and so forth.

Management must recognise that community schools have finite human and physical resources; the school cannot serve everyone in the community, so priorities must be determined.

Schools' communities

The diversity of communities and their subdivisions creates resource management difficulties for community schools. Since their finite resources mean that they are unable to meet all existing needs, defining the community they serve is one stage in the process of establishing priorities. However, once the priority community has been identified the matter of whose needs are to be served will still have to be explored. There are a number of ways this can be done.

First, in a well established community school, management can allow history to dictate who is served. It can continue to meet the needs of those who have traditionally made use of its facilities, encourage the maintenance of the current programme and make incremental changes when and if required.

Second, management in both established or newly developing community schools can let the social market determine who is its community. The schools can make sports facilities available, they can provide adult education programmes, they can organise parent and toddler clubs, they can promote the hire of premises and advertise their social and welfare activities. Those who can afford, or have the self-motivation, to take up the opportunities created by the school will constitute the sector of the community the school wishes to serve.

Third, schools could make a conscious decision about which sectors of the community they can service based upon their resources. Many primary schools, for instance, are committed to meeting their communities' needs, but space and facilities often restrict the schools' scope for development. Consequently, many primary schools focus on parents as the sector of the community they feel they are best equipped to serve.

Fourth, some schools decide to concentrate upon a particular sector of the community either because the school has specialist resources or there is a clear and overwhelming need present in the community. This is often revealed in cases where the school has a system for assessing need which has highlighted a crucial area of demand requiring provision and action.

In addition to being clear about which elements of the community a school serves, it also has to establish which 'products' it has to offer. The 'product range' will also help the school to focus on the sectors of the community which they can effectively serve.

Every community school is different, and this suggests that they are shaped to some extent by their immediate environments and the available skills and technology they have at their disposal.

Activity 3.2   The school's community (R)

A school which has identified its community may derive some benefits from further analysing that community. For instance managers may want to consider how many communities of interest exist within the community the school serves.

This may be followed by considering what the school has to offer as contributions to the life of these communities of interest?

Identifying the school's niche

A community school can carry out product analysis by examining the opportunities it can make available to the community. These opportunities will include the range of premises available. An audit of facilities may be carried out by asking some relatively straightforward questions, including:

- Does the school have

    - a sports hall?
    - a gymnasium?
    - a hall?
    - a theatre or conference facility?
    - a weights room?
    - a bar?
    - a swimming pool?
    - specialist areas?
    - a community or parents' room?
    - squash courts?
    - a drama studio or arts facility?

- Can the school make additional space available for:

    - a community room?
    - a parents' room?
    - a bar?
    - a parent and toddler group?

- Does the school have playing fields?

The product range will be further influenced by the attitude of teaching and non-teaching staff. The auditing procedure can be continued by asking:

- Do we have any designated community education staff?
- Are any staff interested in co-ordinating community education?
- Are any teaching staff interested in
    - tutoring adult education courses?
    - accepting adults in with pupils?
    - involving the community in the delivery of the National Curriculum?
    - providing any community activities?
- What is the attitude of teaching and non-teaching staff to members of the community using the school?
- Are any staff interested in providing out-of-school activities for young people?

The other factors which affect the opportunities the school can extend to the community will include:

- the location of the school in relation to the local community
- the opportunities to attract and generate finance
- the level of contact with the community or in the case of primary schools, with parents
- the availability of volunteers.

An analysis, or audit, of facilities and attitudes allows the school to determine its community 'products' – the range of opportunities that can be made available to the community. Through this process, which can be carried through observation, discussion and interview, management will be in a stronger position to assess which sectors of the community it can effectively serve. It may reveal community education champions among the school staff who just need either the opportunity or encouragement to develop new activities for the community. Equally, there may be blockages or resistance that need to be examined to see if they can be removed or reduced in influence. Often these blockages are restrictions imposed by the school building or by people's attitudes.

Once the school has completed this analysis it will have a clearer picture of the product range that the school can provide.

Assessing need

Assessing need is a key activity in identifying the opportunities and activities which the community requires. Unfortunately, it is a complicated and difficult pursuit, synonymous in many people's minds with surveys and questionnaires. However, as both professional and informed amateur pollsters will confirm, obtaining meaningful opinion from the community is a tricky business.

Although many schools committed to community education spend time attempting to assess community needs, there is a recognition that the results have not always been entirely satisfactory or reliable. When assessing need it is important to realise that community expectations can sometimes be raised. Therefore, realistic targets should always be communicated to the community and the pitfalls of raising false expectations kept in mind.

Community surveys

This usually involves the preparation of a questionnaire which is circulated to homes within the community served by the school. The questionnaire might ask for certain background information about the respondent and asks questions about the kind of activities they would like to see provided at the school in order to meet their needs.

The surveys can be circulated by:

- post
- pupils
- local newspapers
- the school's newsletter.

The positive features of surveys include the following:

- they constitute a genuine attempt being made to assess the need of a wide sector of the community
- they give out the message that the school is interested in the community's needs
- they can provide insight or information about needs that have not been recognised.

Conversely, the negative features of surveys include the following:

- there can be a very low level of response
- questions can be ambiguous and replies misleading
- respondents may answer for others not themselves.

Door-to-door questionnaires

This requires a questionnaire to be prepared and interviewers to be selected and trained in its use. Generally, a selection of homes in the community served by the school are chosen to be visited. However, sometimes questionnaires can be conducted at the school gates with parents or in the local shopping area. Although questionnaires are similar to surveys, because they are conducted by an interviewer they offer the opportunity for clarification about questions and answers, as well as for supplementary questions following up interviewees' responses.

Among the positive features of door-to-door questionnaires are the following:

- face-to-face contact encourages higher level of response
- they offer an opportunity for clarification or follow-up questions
- they contribute towards building contacts.

The negative features of such questionnaires can include the following:

- interviewers must be carefully selected and time is required to train them
- interviewees may give answers that they think the interviewer wants
- door-to-door visiting can be difficult as people may refuse to answer questions or interviewing may be difficult to conduct at times when people are at home.

Focus groups

Marketing organisations have been increasingly using focus groups to obtain opinions about products, services or social policy. This involves selecting a cross-section of people who are likely to have an interest in the product, service or policy area. These people meet as a group and discuss a number of questions posed by the interviewer and their responses are recorded on audiotape or paper. Questions are prepared in advance and an effort is made to ensure that the interviewees invited to the focus group meeting represent a wide cross-section of the community.

The positive features of focus groups include the following:

- they are relatively easy to set up and provide a time-limited opportunity to discuss needs
- they allow for the development of ideas through discussion
- they are generally easy to manage, and with sensitive chairing, they can be kept to task.

The negative features of focus groups include the following:

- they can be dominated by a small number of articulate individuals
- it may be difficult to encourage a true cross-section of the community to attend
- irrelevant issues might begin to dominate the discussions.

Professional hunch

The professional hunch or 'gut-feeling' is a commonly adopted approach to need assessment. This approach still plays a key role in estimating what the community requires and its importance should not be totally devalued. Discussions with experienced community education personnel reveals that their hunch is generally informed by a combination of an accumulation of listening to comments made by members of the community, observation and past experience.

Its positive features include the following:

- it is quick, easy and has few resource implications
- there are no organisational implications
- it does not require additional time or planning.

Its negative features include the following:

- it is not supported by data or quantifiable information
- it depends upon individual perception
- it can reflect personal preference or bias.

Unless comments and experience are recorded it is, however, difficult to represent this professional hunch approach as a systematic assessment of need.

Set it up and see

This is a very action-oriented approach to assessing need, requiring the school to put its hunch into practice and see if the community takes up the activity, course or service. The activity, course or service is promoted and advertised and community take-up is monitored against pre-set targets. Those who do attend are asked to either complete a questionnaire or agree to be interviewed to find out whether the activity is meeting their need and is being held at the right venue, time and in an appropriate form.

The positive features of the 'set it up and see' approach include the following:

- it is not just an idea; it is something tangible which can be used or attended
- contact can be made with the community and provision can be revised or amended according to their responses
- it involves actually doing something, not just talking about it.

The negative features of the approach include the following:

- only the users will be available for interview and the results may therefore be a poor reflection of wider needs
- much time may be spent setting up activities which turn out to be poorly attended
- time must be allowed to pass before a meaningful evaluation can take place.

Persistent listening

Some people believe that need cannot be assessed through a short one-off interview and that a genuine assessment requires familiarity with the community and the interviewee having confidence in those who are assessing their needs. This can only be achieved through a continuous dialogue based upon intensity of listening to the community. In their book *Passion for Excellence* Nancy Austin and Tom Peters (1985) introduce the concept of 'naive listening'. By this they mean listening to people without predetermined expectations about what they are going to tell you. There is always a danger that those assessing need are already anticipating what people are going to want. Naive listening requires the interviewer to remove the filters in their heads, put the professional hunch to one side and just listen to what people say they need. However, this will require a familiarity with the community that will only come with regular and persistent contact. It requires the listener to 'stand in the shoes' of members of the community and really understand what is wanted.

Summary

Effective need assessment is a slippery and elusive concept. If it is to contribute towards the community school's effectiveness, and the needs identified and articulated are to genuinely match the community's real 'wants', assessment will have to be a part of the school's wider ethos. That ethos is one in which the school acknowledges that it is part of the community and attempts to maximise its relationship through open and regular contact informed by mutual respect.

Some management theorists closely associate assessing need with concepts such as 'Management By Walking About' (MBWA). With this approach managers – in this instance school managers – do not tuck themselves away behind desks or become overoccupied with administration, but spend time meeting with community groups and local residents and listening to their perceptions. MBWA rarely comes naturally to managers and this is made worse for school managers by the paradox that, despite schools being public buildings, they are at the same time very private places. Historically, they have offered a cloistered education behind closed doors and managers have tended to be encouraged to exclude the community rather than to include it. This has led to a characteristically unapproachable management style. If community schools are to assess needs accurately, MBWA should be a feature of management strategy.

Any need assessment exercise must guard against raising expectations which the school knows cannot be met. The assessment should not offer an open and unrealistic range of opportunities but should be linked to those which the school knows it can fulfil. If the school overpromises and under-achieves the community may lose confidence in it, and this could adversely affect assessment exercises.

On the other hand, the community should not be offered simply that which is convenient for the school. For example, just because the school finds it has an Italian-speaking teacher on its staff it should not automatically presume the community has a need to speak Italian. There may be a need to learn a language, but it may be one for which the school will have to recruit a part-time adult tutor. The school must achieve a delicate balance between being too prudent and yet not overambitious. Merely providing what suits the school's needs can be almost as damaging to relations with the community as overpromising but delivering nothing. A school should be realistic about its capacity to meet a community's needs, but also be prepared to put itself out a little for the purpose of creating community satisfaction.

Assessing need – dos and don'ts

A number of issues have to be taken into account when assessing needs. For easy reference these are listed below as the dos and the don'ts of need assessment.

Do:

- use a variety of approaches to assessing needs
- have regular contact with key members of the local community
- spend time listening to people
- adopt a Management By Walking About (MBWA) strategy
- use closed or focused questions in surveys as open questions lead to ambiguity and sometimes misleading replies

- be conscious of what you can provide or facilitate and make sure that your interviews or questionnaires identify needs which the school can realistically meet.

Don't:

- expect to identify the community's needs through one-off very occasional assessments
- restrict contact to formal post-holders and officials in the local community
- expect the people you speak to to have immediate opinions
- just aimlessly walk around: you must focus on who you want to observe or listen to
- use questionnaires as the only way to assess needs
- build up false expectations through interviews or questions contained in surveys.

Activity 3.3   Assessing needs (R, T)

In trying to develop a familiarity with need assessment consider assessing need in a very narrow and controlled context. This activity aims to explore the concepts and operational implications of assessing need.

First, think of an area in the school – for instance, a classroom, laboratory, IT room, sports hall, gym, hall or playing field.

Second, choose one of these areas and consider and list the uses it could be put to, to meet a community's needs.

Third, compose three questions that would allow you to elicit answers from the community about how that area could be used to meet their needs. For example, if you choose a laboratory:

'If the school were to offer general science GCSE during the day to adults would you attend the course?' Yes/No
   or
'If a science curriculum workshop were to be offered to you, as a parent, to explain in a practical way what your child was studying would you attend?' Yes/No

Fourth, test the questions on a colleague and see if his or her responses provide information that will assist in assessing need.

Networking

All community schools must develop networks. There is no mystery about networks as they are essentially groups of people who share a common interest or who, for one reason or another, have contact. This contact does not have to be frequent or formalised; in fact Charles Handy, in his book *Understanding Voluntary Organisations* quotes Nancy Foy's law which says that 'the effectiveness of a network is inversely proportional to its formality; it needs a spider, not a chairperson, and a telephone not a schedule of meetings. All successful organisations have good networks' (Handy, 1988, p. 109).

The network operated by a community school has to be both centrifugal and centripetal. While it must be able to establish activities and use the network to promote participation, it must also enable and encourage the activities of other organisations and individuals in the network. Networks have a variety of purposes. They can be used to:

- **Communicate** information about the school's planned activities to potential participants. The most effective form of promotion is by word of mouth. In his book, *Thriving on Chaos*, Tom Peters says that 'innovation takes off only after inter-personal networks have become activated in spreading subjective evaluations' (1987, p. 293). Peters believes that organising word of mouth is important to any organisation's success.
- **Inform** other members of the network of their activities and seek support or resources for the activity. For example, a community education activity may require local authority support and, as a result of networking with them, it may be possible to approach them for assistance. Similarly if the school has networked with local businesses it might also be approached for assistance. Sharing information can also avoid the danger of duplication. By sharing information in the network it might be revealed that someone else is already doing a certain activity. Alternatively, by acting together the effectiveness of an activity could be improved.
- **Assess** community needs as a whole, since isolated attempts to determine needs are rarely effective. Good need assessment is typified by persistence, regular two-way communication and familiarity. A network can provide both consistency of contact and an opportunity for regular and ongoing evaluation of a community's needs.

Effective networking depends upon participants assuming positive and constructive attitudes. Network members should be seen as partners who each have their own aspirations but are willing to work in partnership with others. Networks should be a source of benefits to all its members, so each member should treat others with respect and consideration. The success of any network depends upon being clear as to the reasons for the network and on the quality of the contact. The organisations and individuals that a community school is likely to network with include:

- the local education authority
- other schools in its local cluster or pyramid
- local authority departments – leisure, housing, social services, youth and community services
- colleges of further education
- local businesses
- formal and informal community opinion leaders
- community-based clubs and societies
- Training (or Local) and Enterprise Councils
- places of worship
- local voluntary organisations
- district, town and parish councils.

A number of community schools have strengthened their networking activities by organising a regular, but not necessarily frequent, community lunch which provides a useful opportunity to meet individuals from organisations and the wider community in an informal atmosphere. These lunches generally take a key issue as their focus, but also offer an opportunity for more informal conversation and information-sharing.

Experience shows that meaningful networks take time to develop. They depend on trust, mutual support and, to some extent, friendship and can provide an extremely valuable source of support and information. Schools will probably find that networking is crucial if they want to establish open communications between themselves and their community. As Charles Handy says in *The Age of Unreason* (1989), modern organisations need to be typified by 'telephone wires not fences, pathways not walls'. Networks can make a significant contribution to this end.

Where are we now?

Managers may feel that their school is already 'community-friendly' and well positioned to develop the community dimension. However, it is possible to be unaware of some of the challenges and opportunities that the community dimension can generate. In certain cases, school governors, some senior managers and staff may have mixed feelings about developing the community dimension. There are occasionally those who are strongly opposed to any such developments while others will be extremely enthusiastic about the idea.

A key role of school managers is to decide the degree and the pace at which the school should pursue a community education strategy. When this is agreed managers will have to formulate the precise approach the school needs to take to implement that strategy. This book cannot offer a pre-determined blueprint for the establishment of a community school strategy. As has already been stated, every school is different and schools will find that their approach to the community will be affected by differing factors. The most appropriate place for a school to begin collecting strategic information is from within itself. The school management must understand the organisation as it exists before it plans its community education strategy.

SWOT analysis

One effective technique is to undertake a strategic inventory by preparing a balance sheet of the organisation's strengths and weaknesses. The school will not only need to audit its internal strengths and weaknesses, but will also need to identify those opportunities and threats in the external environment that might have a significant impact upon its activities. This exercise is commonly known as a SWOT analysis, so called because it is designed to identify Strengths, Weaknesses, Opportunities and Threats. However, before carrying out such an analysis management must be clear about purpose on the school's community 'business'. This means going back briefly to first principles and asking what the school is trying to achieve.

This settled, the next task is to detail organisational strengths and weaknesses. The positive side should reflect important skills, knowledge, or resources which can contribute to the school's success in achieving its community education purpose. The negative side should record honestly key limitations that detract from the school's ability to respond to its community.

There are a number of approaches to a SWOT analysis, one of the most familiar being the use of brainstorming in which, using a flipchart, groups of people are asked first to list what they perceive as the school's strengths in terms of developing the community dimension and second, to list weaknesses.

The strengths might include internal factors such as:

- attitude of management
- skills of the teaching staff
- location of school
- attitude of non-teaching staff
- links with parents
- specialist facilities

- zoned heating
- quality of reception area
- existence of school newsletter
- tradition of school usage by clubs/groups
- having community staff
- appropriate financial procedures
- community involvement in the curriculum.

For some schools the strengths listed above could also be weaknesses. For example, certain schools may find that their location is removed from the local community; others may not possess any specialist facilities or staff. Therefore, weaknesses may negatively mirror the list of strengths. Other weaknesses might include:

- lack of space
- absence of funds
- no designated community staff
- high caretaking charges
- poor lighting to main entrance
- no clear access
- no tradition of adult education
- litter around school site
- building in run-down condition.

This analysis should give management a more realistic perspective of the issues facing the development of community education in school. It will point out the foundations on which the school can build and the obstacles which must be overcome. It also allows for the construction of a strategic bridge across which the school may move from its present position to future actions.

Management should not only attach importance to the internal audit, but should also consider the opportunities and threats that exist in the external environment. Opportunities are the positive external factors which the school could use to its advantage. Arguably the number of potential opportunities is limitless, so the manager must restrict analysis only to factors significant to the school's agreed community education purpose. When identifying opportunities it is important to make sure that others are not already meeting, or planning to meet, that need. Generally, a school will wish to avoid duplication and wasting resources, although sometimes it may find itself in a dilemma when it becomes aware that another organisation is making a similar provision, but feels it is in a better position to meet the need more effectively. In order to overcome this dilemma, school management may need to hold discussions with the other providing organisation to explore the possibility for either transferring the provision to the school, or negotiating subtle differences in form or emphasis of provision offered by both organisations.

The opportunities a school may identify include:

- positive support from the local education authority
- a positive attitude in the community towards the school
- absence of any alternative providers or competition
- availability of grants or funding
- leisure services which are seeking new dual-use partners
- a new housing estate being developed.

Threats are negative external forces which inhibit the school's ability to achieve its purpose. Threats can vary in form but may include:

- a local education authority which does not see community education as a school's function
- a further education college which assumes responsibility for all community activities in the area
- an economically disadvantaged community which cannot afford even low-cost activities
- the nearby presence of a local authority-supported leisure centre
- proximity to a purpose-built community school
- reduced LEA funding.

The SWOT analysis should help management identify the key factors which will help the school be successful. It should shape and inform the school's strategy and help it to identify what it can and cannot attempt. Every situation is characterised by a set of controllable variables; management's task is to manipulate those variables to make sure that provision for the community can be secured. The school should take time to establish methods for maximising its strengths, overcome its weaknesses, make the most of its opportunities and minimise the impact of the threats.

Activity 3.4   The internal audit (R, D)

This activity is designed to assist management simulate a SWOT analysis. The activities should be carried out either as a personal brainwriting activity or with staff and governors using more familiar brainstorming techniques. Brainwriting is similar to brainstorming except that it is the individual who writes out a list of words or phrases which they personally feel reflect strengths, weaknesses and so forth. The only equipment required is a single sheet of flipchart paper which should be divided into four quarters with an 'S' written in one corner, 'W' in another and 'O' and 'T' respectively in the remaining two. Write down, in the appropriate section, the school's internal strengths and weaknesses in developing community education and the external opportunities and threats which exist.

If a group approach is preferred, ask colleagues to feed back to one another and list their collective comments under the appropriate heading on the flip-chart paper. Follow up with a discussion as to how strengths can be maximised, weaknesses overcome, opportunities taken and threats reduced.

This discussion could assist the formulation of the school's strategy in developing the community dimension.

Setting objectives

As stated earlier, a school which wishes to further its community dimension has to establish this in its statement of values. However, although the values may influence what each individual in the school believes to be important and consequently have a significant effect on attitudes, these values have to be turned into practice. The initial step in transforming values into practice is to establish objectives. These give the manager targets to aim for and provide a basis for evaluating the success of community education. Without them the manager cannot know where community education is going or how well it is performing.

It is important not to confuse objectives with aims. Aims are broad intentions; they always sit on a point on the horizon and are sometimes never reached. Objectives, on the other hand, are precise. If it can't be measured it is not an objective. The difficulty arises, of course, in that most people only see quantity as measurable. This means that quality can become excluded from the objective-setting exercise. This need not be the case so long as the characteristics or nature of quality are clearly established before setting the objectives.

Before objectives can be established an assessment must be made of the organisation's position. There is little point in setting an objective to increase the number of parents involved in their children's reading if the school does not know how many parents are already involved. Equally, it is of no value to propose raising the level of satisfaction with the way visitors are treated at reception if the school does not know how many visitors are already satisfied.

This means that it is essential for a school to have a pre-agreed scale for measuring the objectives that are set. For example, how does a school define what is meant by parental involvement in their child's reading and what criteria will be applied to its measurement? Does it mean a parent completing a booklet detailing how often they listen to their child? Does listening to a child's reading once every six months amount to involvement? Does it matter what the child is reading to them?

These questions merely serve to highlight the need to clarify objectives carefully. It is also sensible to avoid establishing too many objectives which may tend to overwhelm people. Managers may find it advisable to set a small number – say, five or six – of objectives in key areas. More than this will lead to problems in monitoring their achievement and cause them to become a burden rather than a help.

Well written objectives should conform to the acronym SMART – that is, they should be:

- **Specific**: Objectives should be quantifiable and precise.
- **Measurable**: Managers should be able to plot the organisation's progress towards its objectives; this requires a well defined reference from where to start and a scale for measuring progress.
- **Achievable**: Any objectives that are established should be set with the knowledge that the school has the skills, knowledge and resources necessary for their achievement.
- **Realistic**: There should be sufficient potential human and physical resources and energy to ensure any objective set can be realistically implemented.
- **Time-limited**: Objectives should not only specify what is expected but by when. If an objective is not set within a timeframe its progress is difficult to monitor and evaluating its success is problematic.

The objectives established will be strongly influenced by the community need assessment which will indicate to the school what the community thinks it ought to be doing. The chances of successfully implementing an objective are generally improved when managers involve those responsible for its implementation in setting it.

A community school will usually wish to consider setting objectives in areas such as:

- range of provision
- level of contact and involvement of parents
- number of users
- target groups in the community
- level of income
- number of new activities
- levels of community satisfaction with school
- quality of activities
- management arrangements
- number of examination passes by community students.

Increasingly the type of objectives which a school establishes will have to be set with reference to expectations placed upon it by other organisations. For example, many schools receive funding from their LEA, the provision of which is often dependent upon the school agreeing and achieving pre-arranged targets. Certain LEAs have formalised these targets into Service Level Agreements (SLAs). These agreements are informed by:

- LEA priorities
- previous levels of activity
- school facilities
- need for innovation.

SLAs generally incorporate the four concepts of :

- **effectiveness** – in that LEAs want targets to be established and achieved
- **efficiency** – in that LEAs expect maximum returns from their resource inputs
- **economy** – in that LEAs require schools to apply the concept of value for money to the use of resources
- **equality** – in that LEAs aim to ensure the widest distribution of community education opportunities.

LEAs are not the only organisations that now require pre-agreed objectives to be attached to funding. Many secondary community schools are receiving funding from the Further Education Funding Council (FEFC). Their funding arrangements take into account factors which include:

- special needs
- enrolment figures
- the retention of students recruited to a course
- the number of students who enter for any qualification
- the number of students that obtain the qualification
- the number of students that qualify for remission.

This type of contracting is likely to be extended to other areas of community education activity. Funders will be increasingly looking for measurable outcomes from their investments. Furthermore, the funding organisations are likely to want to play a central role in the specification of these outcomes.

Consequently, two main kinds of objective will have to be considered by managers of schools involved with their community:

1 internally introduced objectives which organisations set for themselves and will allow the school to monitor performance and ensure that plans are being achieved

2   externally specified objectives which permit external funders to evaluate whether resources are being used to good effect and their targets are being achieved.

Activity 3.5   Defining the terminology (R, D)

In order to assist consideration of a development plan for community education it can help to make sure that it is possible to differentiate between:

- aims
- objectives
- goals
- performance indicators?

List or discuss with others what you understand by these words in a management context.

---

4 A living community school

Developing the programme

So far this book has argued that the ethos of the school is the key factor in determining whether a school is justified in considering itself a community school. Values, leadership, working practices and attitudes are the stuff that community schools are made of, not nicely painted school signs or headed school stationery containing the word 'community'. However, Peter Drucker in his book *Managing the Non-profit Organisation* (1990) says that 'the task of the non-profit manager is to try to convert the organisation's mission statement (values) into specifics'. Values, if they are to have any worth, must be capable of being turned into practice. The community education programme of a school committed to, and involved in, its community will be the translation of the school's values into practice.

There is no universally agreed range of activities for a community school. There is no baseline programme, a set of fundamental opportunities, that all community schools have to provide. The belief that a community school can be everything to everyone is clearly just not true. The programme will depend upon opportunity, competence and commitment. A community education programme will contain a broad range of activities which will have been developed as a result of:

- community needs
- available facilities and resources
- leadership
- new opportunities emerging
- expectations of funders
- presence of skills and knowledge.

Each of these factors influencing the programme will be interrelated. For example, the extent to which management will be capable of meeting community needs will be affected by available resources, while the level of resources could be affected by the commitment of leadership.

If, however, a school has adopted a statement of values that contain a commitment to community education, the school will make every effort to ensure its activities respond to its community. The school's community education programme will reflect the community's needs and consequently contain activities for a wide cross-section of the community. These will vary, but are likely to include some of the following:

- provision for the very young
- parent and toddler groups
- nursery provision
- creche facilities
- preschool groups
- out-of-school care facilities
- playschemes
- youth clubs
- youth activities
- scouts, guides, and other voluntary youth organisations
- youth orchestras
- homework clubs
- music, drama and dance groups
- arts and crafts activities
- use of sports facilities
- adult education programme
- senior citizens' clubs
- clubs and associations for the disabled
- day centre provision
- facilities for clinics
- community libraries
- bars.

Managers will have to decide on the most appropriate range of activities for their own school. The type of opportunities the school provides, and the necessary operational arrangements it will need to make, will be influenced principally by local demand and available resources. While there will obviously be variations between schools, management considerations when making provision will be broadly similar. The key issues for management will be:

- location
- organisation

- funding
- legal and technical considerations
- personnel
- resource implications
- marketing and promotion.

For the purposes of attempting to deal with these management issues, provision in community schools is categorised under the headings of:

- early years work
- youth activities
- adult education
- sports and physical recreation
- provision for the elderly
- arts activities
- social activities
- provision for the disabled
- provision for ethnic minorities.

The above categories overlap and, while there are clearly dangers in clustering different provisions in this way, it does indicate the general management issues that have to be taken into account when catering for these sections of the community.

Early years work

This area of work contains a wide range of developments, many of which are associated with the primary sector. These developments are attractive to primary schools as they often do not require additional physical resources. Management of early years work falls into two general areas. The first is to do with the school's organisational policy and the attitude and approach of teaching staff. Aspects of early years work include involving parents in the classroom, home–school visiting by class teachers, visiting parents and children at home before the child starts school and building links with local providers of preschool activities.

The school's management needs to be aware that the success of this kind of work relies upon securing the goodwill and commitment of teaching staff. Teaching is a very private activity and encouraging parents into the classroom therefore requires thorough consultation and discussion with teaching staff. Certain teachers will enthusiastically welcome the opportunity of having parents in the classroom as supporters, associates and extra pairs of hands. Others will be suspicious and anxious about such a development, fearing interference, uninformed criticism and a source of encouragement to gossip about their work. Equally, concepts such as home–school visiting will be embraced wholeheartedly by some teachers while viewed with concern by others.

Management should be sensitive to these and related issues. Developments of these kinds have to be introduced gradually and with willing consent. They will need to be explored through staff meetings and in-service training. Like all innovations, threats should be minimised and benefits maximised.

The second aspect of early years work is still dependent upon teacher attitudes and approaches, but generally has physical resource implications. Parent groups, parent and toddler clubs, activity clubs, creche and preschool groups require physical space. Many primary schools have difficulty in finding accommodation for these types of activity.

While some schools' management can identify excess capacity which can be released for this type of provision, in general, daytime provision is more likely to be found in either purpose-built primary community schools or secondary schools. Of course, the same restrictions on accommodation do not apply outside the school day, although other issues have then to be taken into account, such as caretaking, premises costs and supervision.

The benefits for schools of early years provision include:

- building familiarity and loyalty in the community to a school
- offering support and opportunity for parents to socialise and engage in parent education
- permitting women to participate in daytime adult education and vocational training
- providing for a range of child development activities
- contributing to the variety of activities for young children
- providing childcare facilities for working parents.

Although there are extensive opportunities for providing for early years activities, school management should consider a range of factors when developing them. These factors include:

- the attitude of teaching and non-teaching staff
- the availability of accommodation
- the appropriateness of furniture, equipment and fittings
- facilities for refreshments
- the effect upon the school of adults being on the premises during the day
- the impact on premises costs – heating, lighting, wear and tear
- levels of fees or hire charges
- the attitude of caretaking staff

- arrangements for administering use by parents and adults
- storage of equipment
- legislative issues.

All over the country there exist tremendous examples of good practice in early years provision. Brownsover First School in Rugby has established a valued and popular out-of-school care club. Whitehills Primary School in Northampton has established a highly successful parent-and-child reading session that takes place before the start of every school day. Sutton Manor Community Primary School, St Helens has developed well attended parent education programmes and active home–school links, and West Walker Primary School in Newcastle-upon-Tyne has supported parents through the provision of a community library and a cafeteria operated by parents, as well as a home visiting programme.

Early years work is not restricted to primary schools. Examples of secondary school involvement include: Portslade Community College near Brighton which has established a day nursery; Parkfield School in Wolverhampton which has converted a temporary classroom into a parent and toddler facility and King Edwards School in Morpeth which has provision for young children and their parents each day in its adjoining youth centre. At Cansfield Community High School in Wigan a day nursery, providing facilities for very young children and for after-school activities, has been built with the support of local business.

The extent to which schools are directly involved in the operation and provision of early years activities will vary. Home–school visiting and parents in the classroom obviously require the involvement of the school. However, for some activities, schools assume the role of host or landlord. A school may hire out spare accommodation to a club, group or private company in order to make certain types of activities available. The school may also permit or encourage the local education or health authority, further education college, higher education institution or Open University to make available parent education programmes or child development opportunities. These institutions would be expected to pay a rental to the school for use of accommodation.

Schools which recognise the benefits of closer links with parents and making available early years provision will want to assess need to determine the type of activities they should or could provide.

If ownership of these activities is to be assumed by the whole school it is recommended that staff are involved from the earliest stage. The relationship between parents and the primary school teacher is normally a very strong one. Parents usually feel at ease when coming into school and they are generally on friendly terms with the teachers. Parents of young children accept the importance of coming into school with their child. Of course, there are exceptions to this norm, especially where there is a cultural or language difference or where parents' own experience of school has been particularly unpleasant. In these cases, management will want to pay particular attention to threshold arrangements, including placing special emphasis on greeting parents or by making initial contact. In one primary school in the Midlands which is in an area characterised by multiple disadvantage, the school introduced the idea of taking a gift for the child to their home before the child started school.

The school's management will want to maximise the benefits to be obtained from early years activities and parental involvement. Research has shown that the key influence upon a child's education is parental attitude. The importance of their role could be conveyed to parents through parent education sessions. This could make an important contribution to how parents view themselves in relation to their children's education.

Managers of community education in schools should recognise the political interest in parents and, in particular, in their role as partner in their child's early education. For some years now there has been an unprecedented and growing level of political interest, both within the government and across the major political parties, in the relationships between parents and their children's schools. As teachers well know, this has given rise to a body of new legislation, supported by DFEE and LEA guidelines, for schools to implement.

This legislation has been introduced through a succession of Acts of Parliament (the Education Acts of 1980, 1981, 1986 and 1988). The Parent's Charter which was introduced in 1993 has, among other things, served to summarise these requirements, to extend them in several areas and to give added emphasis to their overlapping, though distinct, concerns.

The legislation of the last decade, including the 'Reporting of Individual Pupil Achievement' regulations of 1990, seeks to strengthen the rights of parents to:

- express a preference as to which school their children shall attend, where this is practicable
- receive information about the school, including information for new and prospective parents and information about the outcomes of assessment of existing pupils
- receive information about their children's work and progress, including a plan of their work within the National Curriculum, an annual written report and specific information about their achievement at the various Key Stages
- participate in the management of their children's schools by becoming elected parent governors and through discussion of the governors' report at their annual meeting, where parents can vote on matters of significance

- be involved, where appropriate, in the assessment and review of special needs provision for their children.

This body of legislation gives emphasis to formal measures of achievement and to the publication of written information. It does not, however, extend the possibilities for an educational partnership between parents and schools.

The implementation of national legislation on home–school relations has placed new demands on teachers and led to developments in professional practice. For example, an assessment of the effectiveness of home–school work is now included in local and national school inspections, and OFSTED inspectors will increasingly seek the views of parents themselves. Similarly, school development plans, which have become a key tool within the planning both of LEAs and of individual schools, now incorporate 'Relations between the school, its parents and the wider community' as a major heading alongside management, curriculum and organisational matters. Many LEAs have also responded to the current situation by setting up working groups and task forces to look into ways in which parents can become involved in such areas as Records of Achievement and reporting to parents.

The requirement to report on the achievements of pupils is attractive to politicians, teachers and parents for different reasons. It presents an opportunity to use some of the untapped interest and potential of parents in this vital area, drawing upon a shared concern to improve the ways in which children's achievements and progress are recognised, recorded and reviewed. This is generally seen as a key educational process in which children and their parents need to be involved if schooling is to be as effective as it needs to be for all of our children.

The Parent's Charter which was produced by government and attempts to summarise the expectations parents should have of schools, emphasises:

- *clarifying rights and obligations*: legal and contractual requirements; professional obligations and the development of good practice; the rising expectation of parents and pupils
- *informing parents*: about their entitlements; about the curriculum and organisation of their children's schools; about changes in the education system
- *providing evidence of performance*: of pupils and teachers; of schools; of the system nationally
- *building and strengthening accountability*: for parents and, in response to the wider public interest, through strengthened monitoring and inspection and through the management of schools.

Recent studies and surveys of parental opinion (increasingly carried out by schools themselves) show that parents are now much more likely to have some sense of their rights and entitlements to information and access, to feel able to express their views, and to become actively involved in their children's education and development.

This growing, though still not universal, sense of entitlement can also be seen in the rapid growth, both nationally and locally, in the number and size of parent organisations of different kinds. Schools seem to have become increasingly willing to utilise the goodwill and practical support which is offered through these organisations. Despite this growth, it is impossible to say precisely what effects recent changes have had upon the expectations and behaviour of parents in relation to their children's schools. This is particularly difficult to estimate because, as studies now show, changes in behaviour nearly always come before deeper changes of underlying attitude.

But it is the combined effects of recent changes that are likely to have the greatest impact. A succession of new laws has strengthened the rights of 'consumers' across the principal public services: relationships between parents and their children's schools have become a dominant concern on the agenda of all political parties, and the media coverage of educational matters to some extent reflects this wider public interest. Finally, there is the evolution and slow spread of a body of practice that is more responsive to the expectations and experience of parents.

Youth activities

Activities for young people initially conjures up an image of youth clubs characterised by pool, table-tennis, snack bars and pop music. However, youth activities come in all shapes and sizes reflecting different tastes and expectations. Youth clubs are a relatively common feature of community school's youth programmes, but they are far from being the only opportunities available to young people.

Traditional youth club work focuses upon activities catering for fourteen year-olds and above, although recently youth work has witnessed a lowering of the average age of its clients, with junior youth clubs offering activities to those as young as eleven.

Senior and junior youth clubs are usually located in secondary schools. In some schools they might have a designated youth wing or separate youth club building. However, in other schools youth clubs are provided in halls, refectory areas, classrooms and sports facilities.

There are a variety of management arrangements for youth clubs. In many instances the staff and premises costs of the clubs are borne by the local authority which consequently often assumes a key role in determining the club's management structure, overall policy and direction. Local authority clubs can have their own separate management committees to whom the club's senior youth worker is accountable. The degree of autonomy a youth club will exercise from the school generally depends upon local authority policy. In some cases where a discrete and influential youth service exists the youth club may be little more than a resident on the school's campus. Alternatively, where an authority has supported an integrated community education policy the youth club may be answerable to the school's community education staff and the youth club management committee could form a subcommittee of the school's governing body.

Community school managers should recognise that youth workers often feel that, where they are an integrated element of a community school, they are treated as a poor relation. Youth workers sometimes suggest that insufficient recognition is given to their work. School management, they claim, do not always understand the purpose of youth work, nor consequently its content or process. Youth club workers can sometimes become the principal target for complaints about misuses of facilities or damage caused to premises or equipment. Youth club client groups can sometimes contain the school's less motivated pupils and therefore become labelled as places where problem pupils congregate.

This is not the sole perspective held by schools about youth clubs or vice versa. Regardless as to whether youth clubs are separate from, or an acknowledged part of, the school there have been some important examples of collaboration, suggesting that, where good working relations exist, it leads to youth clubs having access to school facilities such as sports halls, minibuses, drama studios and specialist areas.

Equally, schools have also found that youth clubs can make an invaluable contribution to the life of pupils and the school by providing:

- lunchtime facilities for older pupils
- outdoor pursuits opportunities
- a different environment for work with disaffected pupils
- an additional range of extracurricular activities.

Recently, the concept of youth activities, or opportunities for young people outside the school day, has been further extended. In the past few years organisations such as Education Extra and Kids Club Network have encouraged both primary and secondary schools to develop in two particular directions. First, schools are being supported in the provision of out-of-school care facilities and, second, to provide after-school activity clubs for their pupils. The out-of-school care clubs have been given additional encouragement by the Department for Education and Employment and by local Training and Enterprise Councils who have provided funding to schools to make available care clubs before and after the school day for children of working parents. The idea is that schools will provide activities so that working parents can have access to affordable and quality childcare at either their children's own school or at one close by.

The idea of after-school activity clubs is being promoted in primary and secondary schools and focuses on giving pupils access to clubs that are devoted to a variety of hobbies or interests, usually taking the form of a sports, arts and craft or science activity.

Other youth activities are also promoted or hosted by schools. These include specialist measures such as homework clubs or 'eleventh sessions'. The latter are periods of extra teaching time during the twilight period of the day. Schools also host youth orchestras, drama companies, sports clubs and voluntary youth organisations such as Brownies, Beavers, Cubs, Scouts and Guides. Schools will assume different levels of responsibility for these activities. In some cases, the school will be given extensive guidance and encouragement by the local authority about making provision available for young people. In other instances the school will simply act as a provider of accommodation. In those cases where youth work is a more integrated element of the school, management will need to consider where it strategically fits in the school's plans.

Youth work often has much to offer, and school management should give it due recognition and attempt to maximise its contribution. The school needs to appreciate the different dimension that youth work provides. Youth work and youth activities in general, do not take the same approach to young people adopted by the school during the day. It has a different culture. Because it is characterised by informal and social education approaches, is non-directive and has different structures and systems to that of the school, different codes of behaviour must be expected. This is not an excuse for unacceptable and anti-social behaviour; it simply means that youth club members who are also pupils at the school cannot be expected to conform to the rules that apply to them during the school day. Since this difference in expectations has the potential to create tensions between the school and the youth club, school managers and youth club workers would be advised to agree an operational framework that clearly spells out how individuals should conduct themselves when they are on-site as a pupil and how they should behave when they are participating in a youth activity.

An additional potential area for disagreement concerns the the use of equipment and facilities. School managers and youth workers should discuss and agree care of equipment and facilities, while also establishing a procedure for dealing with issues that jointly affect the school and the youth club.

Such procedures should also be extended to other youth activities. Quite often there is only limited face-to-face contact between representatives of school and those hiring the school for youth activities. This absence of contact can create the potential for confusion and misunderstanding.

Where youth activities are led by school staff there is often greater clarity about procedures regarding standards of conduct, care of equipment and systems of communication. However, there may still be problems as the member of staff may face a dilemma due to the expectations of school management conflicting with those placed upon them as a youth worker. Activities supervised and led by non-school staff generally encounter no major problems so long as procedures associated with use are clearly agreed in advance.

Much youth work is carried out by volunteers; generally, paid staff are only found in local authority youth clubs. Where the responsibility for paying staff for youth work rests with the school, advice on payscales and conditions of service is available from the local authority or organisations such as the National Youth Agency, Kids Club Network or the Local Government Management Board.

Activity 4.1   Working with young people (R, D)

Youth work forms an important element of a community school's programme and provides a valuable resource to the local community.

There are many ways in which a community school can work with young people outside the school day. This list can be used to audit what is currently being done and help consider what may be developed. Consider what introducing these services would involve.

- breakfast clubs
- out-of-school child care
- playschemes
- homework clubs
- after-school clubs?
- lunchtime youth clubs
- youth club
- Duke of Edinburgh award.

Adult education

Adult education, still commonly referred to as evening classes or night school, forms a central element of many schools' community education programmes. However, the range and scope of the courses shows considerable variation between schools. Furthermore, recent changes in legislation have reclassified adult education into vocational courses (Schedule Two courses) and non-vocational courses. Schedule Two refers to their classification in the Further and Higher Education Act 1992.

Vocational adult education includes all courses that lead to a recognised qualification. Schedule Two of the Further and Higher Education Act 1992 outlines the categories recognised as vocational education courses.

Funding for these courses, and those that are financed by the Further Education Funding Council (FEFC), is based upon a specified formula. Schools cannot make direct application for funding from the FEFC but have to enter into a relationship with a sponsoring body, normally a college of further education. In certain cases the LEA coordinates the schools' applications to FEFC, but in others schools approach a college of further education directly to make the application on its behalf. Schools are not restricted to working with local colleges, but many find it more convenient to request that their local college acts as their sponsoring college.

Vocational adult education courses are usually provided in the evening, but some courses are provided during the day where schools have available accommodation. A number of schools such as Bodmin Community College, Paignton Community College and TP Riley Community College, Walsall, operate off-site annexes which accommodate a wide selection of daytime vocational courses, while some schools – for example, Whitby Community College in North Yorkshire and Cranford Community School in Hounslow – operate extensive daytime programmes on their school site.

Non-vocational (non-Schedule Two) adult education courses come in a variety of shapes and forms in community schools. Many community schools provide an LEA-funded adult education programme which is either directly managed, administered and supervised by the LEA's adult education services or by the local college of further education in those cases where the LEA has delegated the provision of non-vocational adult education to colleges. In some LEAs the budget for non-vocational adult education has been delegated to community schools. Where this has occurred the administration and supervision of adult education becomes the responsibility of the school. This delegation is usually accompanied by a Service Level Agreement (SLA) which indicates the level of adult education provision the LEA expects and is specified in terms of content, hours, quality and recruitment. Penalties can be incurred by the school if it is unable to achieve the appropriate level of service detailed in the SLA.

Where schools operate LEA-funded adult education programmes the LEA generally provides guidance on such matters as:

- fees
- fee concessions
- minimum levels of recruitment
- tutors' salary scales
- length of course sessions
- length of terms.

Non-vocational adult education courses generally take place on weekday evenings from about 7.00 pm and last for between one and a half and two hours. It is not uncommon for terms to be ten weeks long, and courses are provided for two, and sometimes three, terms. Student attendance decreases during the summer term which is why some LEAs only offer courses in the autumn and spring terms.

LEAs encourage experimentation with adult education. This has resulted in innovatory approaches being promoted which include short taster courses, one-day specialist courses, and daytime courses aimed particularly at the elderly or women.

In addition to LEA-financed non-vocational adult education a wide range of other providers exist. There are courses offered in schools by:

- the Workers' Educational Association (WEA)
- extra-mural departments of universities
- the Women's Institute.

Adult education courses may also be provided by private organisations, especially popular courses that attract substantial numbers of participants such as keep fit, yoga, aerobics and ballroom dancing. The school hires its facilities to these organisations and, in return, they pay a letting fee to the school. The tutor's fee comes from the charge made to course members.

There are examples of community schools which provide their own adult education courses. Such adult education programmes have to be either self-financing, or funding has to be obtained from an organisation other than the LEA or FEFC. The absence of LEA regulations sometimes results in greater flexibility in terms of minimum levels of recruitment, tutors' salaries and fee structures. One obvious disadvantage of a self-financing programme is that it makes the provision of fee concessions for those on benefit or unwaged difficult. However, careful book-keeping can sometimes permit some fee concessions if a balance can be maintained between the numbers of full-fee payers and those receiving concessions. A self-financing adult education programme is only viable in areas where there are sufficient people who can afford full fee; it is rarely viable in disadvantaged areas. In addition, formal and traditionally structured non-vocational adult education has a poor track record in disadvantaged communities. In these areas adult education often has to take a more informal and negotiated form and be based upon the concerns and preoccupations of local people. Courses in these areas aim to incur the lowest possible costs and are consequently usually held during the day and led – if led at all – by volunteers.

Adult education is not exclusively located in secondary schools. Primary schools do have adult education programmes, but they are usually less extensive. A significant restriction on adult education in primary schools is the facilities which raise fundamental problems such as the size of furniture or availability of materials and equipment. Primary schools which have community or parents' rooms do have adult-sized furniture and can obtain equipment, but in primary schools where the building design is open-plan the opportunities for adult education are further reduced because of security problems.

Sports and physical recreation

Along with adult education, sport is a central element of community education programmes, particularly for those in secondary schools. The community sports programme in some schools has assumed such dimensions as to have overshadowed other elements of community education. Sport, however, is less significant in primary schools because few have appropriate facilities, although many do hire out their halls for sports such as badminton, judo and gymnastics. Sports activities are attractive to the community. The Sports Council reports that participation in both indoor and outdoor sport has increased in the past ten years. The Council has been strongly committed to extending sporting opportunities and, as a consequence, has taken an active role in promoting community use of schools' sports facilities.

There are a variety of different arrangements for the management and organisation of community sport in schools. The most basic form is where school sports facilities are hired out to a sports club, association or local authority sports course. In these cases the school management's responsibilities involve taking the booking and ensuring that the building is open, lit and heated. Members of the club, association or course are responsible for supervision, conduct and use of equipment.

Another approach to sports provision is a dual-use agreement with the leisure services department of either the metropolitan authority or, in shire counties, with the district council. School governors can negotiate an agreement with leisure services about the use of premises that apportions responsibility for managing community use of sports facilities. These agreements will include:

- times of day when leisure services will assume responsibility
- days of the week when leisure services will be responsible
- the situation with regard to use at weekends and school holidays
- responsibility for staffing, booking arrangements, promotion of facilities, maintenance and equipment
- range of facilities included in the agreement.

A mechanism for dealing with disputes will also be necessary.

There are enormous variations in the types of dual-use agreements. In some, leisure services assume complete responsibility for the management, administration and staffing of recreational provision outside the school day. This might even extend to the leisure services department being the principal funder of the sports facilities. At the other extreme, the leisure services department may make a grant to cover some element of the costs associated with either capital or revenue expenditure.

The degree to which a community school proactively develops a sports programme depends upon the school's policy and the resources it decides to dedicate to community sport use. In some community schools they not only react to demand from the community, but also actively promote use of the sport facilities. This includes organising their own courses, groups and instruction sessions. Schools which proactively meet community sports needs and sports development usually appoint a member of staff with responsibility in this area. This person may be a member of the school staff or may be an additional part- or full-time appointment.

Sport features in the programme of most schools interested or involved in their community. This takes a wide variety of forms from the occasional let to a keep fit group through to a seven-day-per-week, 52 weeks-per-year programme. The range of sports offered by community schools is considerable and reflects the facilities it has available.

Community use of sports facilities not only makes efficient use of premises – which if not used by the community would be empty and a possible target for vandalism – but also provides a valuable source of income. Many schools have superb facilities that rival those found in leisure centres. Unfortunately the management by the school of their sports facilities is not always as efficient as it should be. This situation can be improved by schools obtaining advice on the management of sports facilities from the local authority leisure services department. Careful thought should be given to the management of recreational facilities, with particular consideration being given to:

- length of sessions
- start and finish times of each session
- balance between private hire and casual public use
- systems and staffing for booking facilities
- rational use of space.

Creative approaches to management can generate considerable income from the hire of sports facilities. This income can make it possible to support and subsidise other activities that do not create surplus income – this is sometimes referred to as the 'Robin Hood Principle'.

Many schools have a wide range of sports facilities including:

- sports halls
- gymnasiums
- playing fields
- halls
- all-weather surface – sometimes with floodlighting
- squash courts
- tennis courts
- athletics tracks
- multi-gyms.

Some schools have introduced sunbeds and jacuzzis for community use. Swimming pools are also a feature of some schools, but these require specialist and informed management if they are to be used effectively. Schools with swimming pools can obtain considerable benefits from a dual-use arrangement with leisure services which have the technical expertise to manage and maintain the pools. However, schools are likely to want to negotiate conditions of any agreement with leisure services to ensure that such agreements lead to mutual advantage. In some schools an agreement has been reached with the district council which divides responsibility for financing the staffing and supervision of public use of the pool from maintaining the building and equipment.

Capital finance for sports facilities can come from a number or combination of sources including:

- the local education authority
- the leisure services department
- the Sports Council and the Lottery
- the parish council
- a voluntary sports club or governing bodies of sport
- local fundraising
- charitable foundations
- industry and commerce.

TP Riley Community School in Walsall has well developed sports facilities which are an example of joint funding from the LEA and the Sports Council. Bridgemary Community School in Hampshire, a former winner of a Sports Council award for management of sports facilities, had its facilities largely financed by the district council. An example of the contribution which town councils can make can be found at Holyrood Community School which has benefited from Chard Town Council support, while Callington School in Cornwall has developed first-class facilities as a consequence of cooperation between a voluntary foundation, the district council and the county council.

Use of school facilities for sport, which has long been a government policy objective, is not restricted to secondary schools. Many primary schools host activities in their halls, on their playing fields and, for those that have them, in their swimming pools. Certain primary schools, such as Whitehall Community School in Walsall and Feldon School in Warwickshire, have had their facilities enhanced to make community sports use feasible.

The benefits of use of schools sports facilities is reflected in terms of:

- greater efficiency in use of facilities
- building stronger ties with the community
- generating income
- improving quality of life and standards of health in the local community.

There are, however, other issues to consider that can be regarded as obstacles to be overcome, such as:

- caretaking costs
- additional cleaning
- costs of management and administration of use of facilities
- quality of changing facilities, car parking and social areas
- additional wear and tear on equipment and facilities
- excessive use of playing fields
- conflicts with the school's needs, including use of sports hall for examination purposes
- additional storage for equipment.

These issues will need to be tackled, but they are all problems capable of resolution as can be testified by the current extensive use of facilities. However, finding solutions will require forethought and negotiation.

A further key component to achieving effective use of sports facilities is the attitude of the physical education staff. Their passive support is, of course, essential, but their active support can make an enormous contribution to the successful development of community use. Management should be sensitive to the attitude of PE staff and discuss thoroughly with them any concerns they may have about community use. Involving PE staff directly in community use has a number of advantages, but if this is not possible arrangements must be made for communication between users and school PE staff. To encourage PE staff involvement incentives could be offered, such as purchasing additional equipment or enhancing the PE department's capitation from income generated through community use.

John Nisbet said in his book on community education in the Grampian Region of Scotland, entitled *Towards Community Education* (1981), that schools can be like football grounds, used only for short periods and lying empty and unused for the majority of the time. Schools sports facilities, managed appropriately, provide an extremely valuable local contribution to a community's health, welfare and recreational opportunities.

Provision for the elderly

It is vital that the community school's management do not stereotype their community, and this is particularly important when considering the needs of senior citizens and retired people.

This group is becoming an increasing large proportion of the community. In the period 1983–2003 the number of people of 75 years or older will increase by nearly 10 per cent. It is interesting to compare statistical trends between now and the beginning of the century. In 1900 there were barely more than 10 000 people aged 90 years or over – one in every 3500 of the population. Today, there are more than 250 000 people over 90 or one in every 225 of the population. Similarly, in 1900 out of every 100 people, 31 were under 16, 64 were 16–64 and five were over 65. Today, out of every 100 people, 20 are under 16, 64 are 16–64 and 16 are over 65 years.

Furthermore, people are now living active lives for longer, rather than just existing. People remain ambulant and mentally active for many years after they retire. In his book, *The Age of Unreason*, Charles Handy (1989, pp. 34–9) discusses the changing shape of work, and from the analysis he carries out it is possible to conclude that from once being a 47-47-47 society in the early 1960s – that is, we worked for 47 years of our lives for 47 weeks a year and 47 hours per week – today, we have become a 37-37-37 society, working 37 years of our lives for 37 weeks a year for an average of 37 hours per week. The indications from his book are that this is likely to reduce further as more employment becomes part-time, so that by the millennium the statistics are likely to suggest that we will work for only 25 years of our lives with weeks and hours being determined by whether we work full-time or part-time.

In essence, this means people are retiring earlier and still have considerable physical and mental energy. Community education can tap into this in two ways. It can either harness the energy of the retired and use their skills and knowledge in a paid or voluntary capacity to deliver community education. Alternatively, it can make provision for the retired through clubs, activities and courses.

Many senior citizens and retired people will participate in mainstream community education activities, although, because they no longer work, they may want to participate in these activities during the daytime and at weekends.

Management in community schools might find a classification of retired people developed by the Association of Metropolitan Authorities (AMA) helpful. They refer to elderly people as the old elderly or the young elderly. The prefix has nothing to do with chronological age, but refers to the physical and mental capacity of elderly people.

The young elderly are those people who are ambulant and are not subject to mental disability. The old elderly are those people who are either physically or mentally incapacitated or both.

The majority of retired and elderly people can be categorised as young elderly. They should not be seen as a sector that has to be cared for; rather, they should be seen as people to be empowered. Community education offers a strategy for empowerment. Many retired and elderly people will make use of mainstream intergenerational provision in community schools such as adult education, sports activities and special interest groups. However, as they may have similarities in terms of experiences, they may also want opportunities to meet together, at specific times. Friendship patterns often exist within generations as opposed to across them, so the opportunity to socialise and mix should also be made available. Therefore, in addition to participating in intergenerational activities, retired and elderly people may also wish to participate in the University of the Third Age and daytime adult education. Examples of the active and extensive University of the Third Age programmes can be found at Thomas Bennett Community College in Crawley and Bretton Woods Community School in Peterborough.

There might also be a demand for:

- lunch club facilities
- meeting rooms for self-managed social clubs
- specialist adult education courses tailored to older people's requirements.

Community schools also aim to respond to the needs of the old elderly, usually in collaboration with one or more other agencies. For example, some schools provide rooms which are used as day centres. The furniture and transport is financed by a voluntary organisation such as Age Concern or Help the Aged and/or by the local health authority or social services departments. Examples of day centres in community schools can be found in Harrow Way School in Andover and at the Dukeries in Ollerton, Nottinghamshire. There are also examples of community schools which work with the LEA to provide outreach adult education courses in homes for the elderly. In these cases the school recruits the part-time adult tutor, arranges the course in conjunction with the warden of the home and takes responsibility for its administration. The LEA pays the tutor's salary.

Finance can have a significant influence on work with retired and elderly people. They may not have the same level of purchasing power that they once possessed and could be entirely dependent on a pension. Consequently they will require remission of fees if they are to participate in activities. The full cost of activities cannot be passed on to retired and elderly people and, therefore, additional income must be attracted from elsewhere to provide the necessary subsidy. This can be obtained from another agency such as the LEA, local authority, health authority, social services, or a charity, trust or foundation. Alternatively, funding might be effected by means of an internal cross-subsidy through which an activity generating a surplus can be re-directed to underwrite one that does not.

Activity 4.2   Education for all (D, T)

There can be both psychological and physical restrictions to participating in community education in school. Schools interested in working with their communities should aim to reduce all those factors limiting participation. Consider what evidence exists to demonstrate a community-friendly school.

- Are there external signposts?
- Are there internal signposts?
- Is reception a window, a desk or a counter?
- Do you have ramps?
- Are there notices in mother-tongue languages?
- Do you advertise your activities in the local free paper?
- Are all areas of the school accessible to older people or people with disabilities?
- Do you have a community sports/arts policy?
- Do you have refreshment facilities for the community?
- Does your insurance cover community use?

Once this activity has been completed it may be useful to consider whether your present arrangements further community access.

Arts activities

Community schools can be important venues for the arts. Schools such as Oulder Hill in Rochdale and Alumwell in Walsall have impressive theatre facilities which attract performances from professional and amateur theatre companies. Few community schools have these purpose-built facilities, but this has not restricted their role in promoting the performing arts. Community schools extend use of their drama studio to amateur companies for rehearsals and these and other facilities are made available for performances. An increasing number of schools have dance facilities, such as those found in Littlehampton Community School in West Sussex, which are hired out for dance classes, dancing schools and dance workshops. Schools make contributions to community arts in other ways. For instance, many schools hire out rooms to local rock bands for practice, while others make available music rooms for people wishing to practise a particular instrument.

School halls which have stages are used for plays, concerts and dances, while schools with specialist accommodation, such as Horndean with their excellent Barton Hall, use their facilities as the venue for arts festivals.

In addition, a number of schools have community libraries, stocked for, and accessible to, school students and members of the community. School management will find that the arts is rarely a source of income generation but can contribute enormously to a school's profile and image. The arts can also play a valuable part in promoting intergenerational activities. People, both young and old, can be drawn together on arts projects whether for such events as a community play or an orchestral concert. Of course the arts have value in themselves but, in terms of management, they can make a useful and important contribution to marketing and promotion.

Here is an example of a school's community arts policy that is taken from Horndean Community School near Portsmouth:

Arts Policy – Horndean Campus

The philosophy: The Horndean Centre seeks to offer the highest quality arts education, recreation and leisure opportunities for the benefit of the community. It works in partnership with local people enabling them to determine relevant arts needs. The Horndean Centre also works in partnership with Hampshire County Council, East Hampshire District Council and Horndean and Clanfield Parish Councils.

Aims: to make educational, cultural, recreational and leisure arts provision for the local residents and students of the school; to involve local people in the process by which this arts provision is made and developed; to provide the maximum arts facilities, equipment information and a programme of events; to act as an arts centre for the wider area.

Theatre and drama

The new Barton Hall auditorium provides a large facility seating 450. It has good acoustics, an excellent sound and lighting system and easily accessible controls in a purpose-built control box. It also has a spacious foyer and a bar. With good rehearsal facilities for drama, provision will include youth theatre and drama workshops, specialist classes in performance skills, lighting, make-up and costume. The facility lends itself well to a community drama festival.

Music

There is a strong local tradition, within the school and the community, with orchestras and bands, pop groups, jazz clubs and choral associations. The Barton Hall is an ideal space for large-scale music works with ample performing space and superb acoustics. Barton Hall will allow for regular performances by professionals and amateurs, with opportunities for specialist tutors and companies to visit. A community music week is planned with Bournemouth Symphionetta. The festival will involve other schools, local choral and music groups, churches and community centres as well as the Horndean Campus.

Dance

The Barton Hall is used for dance and there is also access to the gym and sports hall which gives the Campus a wide range of spaces for large- or small-scale dance events. Youth dance began to develop some years ago and the BT Youth Dance Festival is now held at the Barton Hall. Professional touring companies are being introduced, especially those companies that provide specialist tuition and workshops. With the Community Partnership Grant from BT and Barclays New Futures, a special needs dance worker has been appointed to work on campus as part of East Hampshire District Council's Danceability programme. A series of taster days of different types of dance are planned, including contemporary, jazz, Flamenco, Egyptian and traditional. Community country and western, rock and roll and jive dance festivals are held on the campus.

Visual arts

The new foyer provides a high quality community arts gallery and exhibition area and can accommodate a wide variety of exhibitions. Local amateur and professional artists, special needs groups, local schools and colleges hold exhibitions. Local photographic societies, painting and ceramics groups, exhibit and use the campus for meetings and classes. Guest artists and tutors are provided on a short-term of residency basis.

Film

There is no local cinema or film society. A projection gallery is included in the Barton Hall along with raked seats for 250. The venue would provide a good base for the showing of films. A small film committee is planned and could be responsible for bookings, programming and publicity. A wide range of films could be screened, as well as screening educational films for schools, colleges and special interest groups. Advice is being sought from Southern Arts Film and Video Officer and contact is being made with other local film societies.

Social activities

It was no coincidence that Henry Morris dubbed the community schools in Cambridgeshire 'village colleges'. He wanted the schools to become the focus for the village community, not only for educational and recreational pursuits, but for social purposes too. This dimension has been subsequently seized upon, throughout the country, by schools involved in their community.

Schools have become the venue for all kinds of social and celebratory events including wedding receptions and birthday parties. Many also provide facilities for:

- quiz nights
- discos
- presentation evenings
- social functions
- exhibitions
- trade shows
- conferences.

Hiring out facilities for social events has the potential for generating large sums of money, but there are a number of management issues arising from this type of use.

First, some users want access to catering facilities. In some local authorities, regulations may only permit use of kitchens if a member of the school meals service is present. This may affect the attractiveness of using school premises.

Second, some social events can become high-spirited and have, on occasions, resulted in misuse of equipment and premises. Consequently some schools have introduced deposits or caution money to cover themselves in the case of damage or misuse.

Third, some schools have bars which have to be managed and stocked. This requires specialist staff who must be present when the bar is open. Furthermore, it may be necessary to establish a separate legal status for the bar to conform with charity law and Inland Revenue requirements. Permanent or occasional licences for bars also need to be obtained. Magistrates around the country interpret licensing regulations differently. Also, the number of occasional licences an applicant can have each year can be subject to restriction, and special licensing conditions can be attached to bars in schools. Examples of where excellent and well established bars can be found are at Thomas Estley Community College in Leicestershire and Richard Aldworth School in Basingstoke .

Fourth, social events sometimes require caretakers or building superintendents to open and lock buildings at unsociable hours, and not all will want to do so on a regular basis. Arrangements for building supervision for such events must be established with the caretaker prior to accepting bookings.

Fifth, a school must make sure that its insurance policy covers social activities and that adequate guidelines are prepared for users of school premises. The school will also need to agree a scale of charges for the hire of premises and use of facilities.

Sixth, to attract and to maintain use of premises for social activities, the school may have to upgrade and improve its facilities. As it will be competing with other providers of social amenities, it will have to give careful thought to the decor and the appearance of areas to be used for social activities. There are schools which have designated adult or community lounges, and these are styled and furnished to reflect an adult atmosphere. These are often areas that are hired out for social events as they provide attractive and comfortable surroundings.

Provision for the disabled

Community schools are committed to enriching the lives of all the people in their community. To make sure that this entitlement is extended to disabled people, schools should pay particular attention to access.

Although there is no stereotypical disabled person, provisions which are regarded as generally beneficial for the disabled include:

- **Ramps.** These provide access for people in wheelchairs and avoid the use of steps by other disabled people who may not require wheelchairs but face mobility problems.
- **Lifts.** The provision of lifts permits greater access to all of the school's facilities and enables disabled people to use facilities above the ground floor. The existence of lifts in schools such as Colton Hills in Wolverhampton and Connah's Quay in Deeside makes it possible for disabled people to gain access to specialist resources on all floors of the building.
- **Toilets.** The location of toilets for the disabled needs careful consideration, but it goes without saying that such a facility is essential if use by disabled people is to be encouraged.

Provision for disabled people in community schools does not stop at issues of access to buildings. Consideration also needs to be given to equipment. Disabled people may encounter difficulty, for instance, in using standard computers, tools, cutlery or drinking utensils. Schools that wish to make appropriate provision ought to discuss these issues with social services, health personnel or the appropriate local authority officer.

A number of community schools provide accommodation for clinics, clubs and day centres for disabled people. These offer important opportunities for people with and without disability to mix. There are schools which have purpose-built facilities for clinics or day centres, such as Sutton Centre in Nottinghamshire and Frankley Community School in Birmingham. There are other schools which have converted facilities to enable use by the disabled.

Provision for ethnic minorities

Where schools serve ethnic minority communities, their community education programmes are significantly influenced by their needs and expectations.

Community schools are sensitive to different cultural and ethnic group requirements and this is reflected in their provision. Two community schools in Leicester – Hazel Street and Moat Community College – offer an example of the type of programmes that community schools serving ethnic minority communities can provide. As well as recognising the need to offer adult education courses that address their interests, the schools also recognise and respect cultural considerations such as making available provision for women only. They encourage local organisations to arrange their own activities by providing accommodation yet still offer support when requested.

Community schools aim to celebrate ethnic diversity through all aspects of school life. The school curriculum draws upon the richness of the cultures found in their community, including opportunities for exhibitions of dance, art and cultural festivals. Pupils see, read and learn about different ethnic groups and their traditions.

This commitment to cultural development extends beyond pupils at the school. Courses are organised for the adult community in cookery, the arts and music.

Schools serving communities where the population contains a high proportion of non-English speakers ensure their information and advertising materials are written in community languages. Furthermore, they appreciate that ethnic minority communities welcome the opportunity to organise and manage provision and, as a result, work collaboratively with groups representing specific ethnic minorities who organise and administer their own programmes.

Community schools also provide venues for religious and cultural events. They provide locations for:

- places of worship
- weddings and birthday parties
- community meetings
- cinema.

A number of community schools offer accommodation for other activities including:

- community languages courses
- religious instruction
- clubs for the elderly.

School managers should be aware that ethnic minority communities may be even more reticent about using community schools than people from the majority community. As cultural differences may constitute an extra barrier to participation, schools should try to be particularly proactive. They must send out the right messages to the ethnic minority community. Thought must be given to use of language, images and other forms of communication. Links should be formed with representatives of ethnic minority groups and encouragement should be given to these groups to use the school to organise their own provision.

Schools should examine the profile of their community staff and aim to employ people from ethnic minority groups. Managers should survey usage and make sure that it at least reflects the community's ethnic profile. School management should also be sensitive to cultural issues. For example:

- signposting should be in community languages
- it may be necessary to make available daytime provision for women, and ensure that it remains 'women only'
- adult education tutors and part-time youth workers should be recruited from among ethnic minorities
- refreshments served in the school's community refectory or cafe should acknowledge cultural traditions.

People, regardless of ethnic background, will want access to the whole range of opportunities provided by the community education programme. For ethnic minority groups, accessing the programme may depend on the school sending out positive messages to the community and making provision which is differentiated and specific to their interests and lives.

Activity 4.3 Analysing your school's community education programme (R, T)

This activity provides an opportunity to consider individually, or with all the appropriate staff and personnel, the range and scope of the school community education programme and the feasibility for developing the programme.

	Yes/No	If no, what factors prevent making provision?	If the school would like to make provision how might this be achieved?
Does the school provide the following in its programme:			
Parent and toddler groups?			
Out-of-school care activities?			
Provision for ethnic minorities?			
Creche facilities?			

	Yes/No	If no, what factors prevent making provision?	If the school would like to make provision how might this be achieved?
Provision for disabled people?			
Youth activities?			
Social activities?			
Adult education?			
Sports activities?			
Provision for elderly people?			
Arts activities?			

5   School and the community

Pupils and community schools

The concept of integrated community schools has been mentioned several times earlier. These are schools which recognise that, first and foremost, they must educate pupils of statutory age, but see this as part of a lifelong education process. The integrated community school sees itself as a provider of lifelong learning opportunities, and the community permeates school life.

In the integrated community school, community education values can be seen to be informing the whole organisation. In the integrated community school, values are lived out in hard evidence, as well as in fine words about community education throughout the school. The concept of the integrated community school is rigorously put to the test when schools are asked to demonstrate where community education can be found in the mainstream of the organisation.

Pupils form a crucial part of any school community, but all too often are given low priority on the list of community education client groups. Schools that want to take maximum advantage of community education must ensure that its benefits are experienced by their own pupils. Schools play a key role in preparing pupils for adult life and the community dimension can greatly enrich that process.

Community education, when applied to mainstream schooling, takes a variety of forms. This chapter outlines some of the ways it is interpreted and the benefits for pupils and the wider community.

Parents as partners

There are powerful reasons, which add up to a convincing case, for teachers to involve parents as much as possible in the education of their children. They include the following:

- Parental support leads to greater achievement by their children.
- Parents are entitled to information and access.
- Parents have skills which they can bring to their children's education.

Schools acknowledge parents' role as the first and continuing educators of their children and recognise that they have much to gain through drawing on parents' unique knowledge of their own child and through enlisting parental support. This can lead to teachers and parents working together to give children the best possible education.

In recent years legislation and ensuing regulations have sought to strengthen the parents' rights. Parents now possess rights to:

- express a preference as to which school their child shall attend
- receive information about the school
- receive information about their child's education and progress
- participate in the management of their children's schools.

Parents, however, need to be more than vicarious consumers of education – the relationship with the school ought to extend much deeper. A wide range of school-based initiatives have been implemented to encourage parents not to see themselves, nor be seen by the school, merely as consumers of services delivered by schools and teachers. However, it is much easier to talk about partnership than actually make it happen. Management clearly perceive parents as partners and have the competence to translate it into practice.

There are different perspectives about partnership, and it has to be accepted that not all partnerships have to be on an equal basis. Partnerships would probably be understood as:

- sharing responsibility and ownership
- a degree of mutuality
- shared values, or at least a mutual respect for others' values
- joint action.

The task facing management is how to continue to develop acceptance of, and the practice of, involving parents as partners.

The case for parents as partners must be made to teachers in the school if the aim is to work towards genuine partnership. Management will have to encourage teachers to identify the benefits of working with parents. The challenges of a partnership approach should not be ignored, but the central requirement for building partnerships has to be a positive disposition to work with parents among the teaching staff. The benefits of partnership include:

- shared learning opportunities in the home and school
- knowledge of, commitment to and involvement in, the school curriculum
- acknowledging the home as a crucial element in children's learning
- support for children's learning in the home
- developing children's self-esteem which can contribute positively to their learning.

Making contact with parents requires thought and planning. Appropriate styles of communication have to be considered. Communication is a complex issue. It is easier to discuss the means of communication than it is to discuss its effects. It is also important to bear in mind that communication is a two-way process involving listening as well as talking. Managers must consider:

- the purpose and style of a school's communications
- its frequency, timing and coordination
- the attractiveness of written communications
- the means available for producing written communications
- how and why teachers speak to parents.

Managers should also review parents' impressions of communication methods. Do they feel it:

- is effective?
- conveys sufficient information?
- is presented in an appropriate style?

In addition, parents need to be consulted about the ways they are addressed, welcomed and generally treated. The quality of communications will significantly influence the development of partnerships. In looking at developing its partnerships with parents a school will explore all the strategies open to it. These will include the following:

- **Social activities** aimed at breaking down the barriers including quiz evenings, jumble sales, car boot sales, parents sports teams and so on.
- **Support activities** aimed at encouraging parents to support the school. This typically involves Parents' Associations and fundraising events.
- **Curriculum-sharing activities** which help parents gain insight into the curriculum.

- **Decision-making activities** aimed at encouraging parents to contribute to the school's decision-making processes. These take a variety of forms but include annual parents' meetings and class meetings whereby the parents of the children in each class meet once a term to discuss developments in the school.
- **Adult learning activities** targeted at parents themselves.
- **Annual parent–governor meetings** used to promote partnership approaches and explore its benefits and practical implementation.

This is not an exhaustive list of activities to promote partnership with parents, it simply illustrates a range of strategies.

Schools with red lines drawn across the school playground accompanied by the sign 'Parents are requested not to go beyond this line' may exist. However, schools do not require 'red lines'. The ethos of some schools can prove a sufficient deterrent to parental involvement. Attitudes are the crucial factor influencing the promotion of effective partnerships. Managers need to promote positive and responsible attitudes among staff and parents. Schools may wish to explore the introduction of ground rules, for both teachers and parents, which will guide and establish conditions for effective partnership.

For teachers

- Consider the welcome you offer children and parents.
- Be flexible and attempt to respond quickly to individual parents.
- Be understanding of parent's predicaments and circumstances.
- Consider your style and manner of communicating.

For parents

- Acknowledge the role of teachers.
- Recognise teachers' knowledge and skills.
- Consider your style and manner of communication.
- Show consideration regarding the issues which teachers encounter in the classroom.

Responsibility for creating the conditions for developing effective partnerships with parents lies with management. Teachers must be supported in developing work with parents. Managers should consider issues of:

- time for teachers to meet parents
- restraints placed upon teachers by the timetable
- traditional attitudes which inform teacher–parent relationships

- cultural misunderstanding – economic as well as ethnic and religious
- personal safety of staff
- responsibility for planning work with parents.

The key to partnerships with parents is the school's values. Time and opportunity must be made for planning the development of those values which reflect the importance of partnership and the identification of strategies for turning these into practice.

Activity 5.1   Parents and schools: who benefits? (R, D, T)

It may help the school if it catalogues current/recent work on partnership with parents and looks at the purpose of this work.

Think of all the parent partnership work that the school has been involved in over the past six months and consider this in terms of benefits. For example, some work is aimed at benefiting the parent's own child (for example, parental involvement in reading, or IMPACT maths), whereas other work is aimed at benefiting the school in general (for example, parents running the book shop or helping in the classroom), and yet other work is aimed at benefiting the parents themselves (for example, informal education groups for parents, or counselling). Try to link the partnership work in which the school has been involved and record who have been the beneficiaries.

This should lead to a general consideration focusing on the following questions:

- How consistent is our parent partnership work throughout the school?
- Who are the main beneficiaries?
- How can we strengthen our parent partnership work?
- How does our current work with parents link with our statements about the meaning of partnership?

Home–school links

Schools still retain some of the vestiges of their past; there still exist traces of their former remoteness. Schools once perceived themselves as havens of learning, a place where children could detach themselves from the rest of their lives. High walls and heavy doors presented an image of privacy and 'other-worldliness'. Pupils were cloistered away and shielded from contaminating influences.

To this day teaching remains a very private affair. Schools can easily restrict the overt intrusions of the wider community. Indeed, the often unpleasant memories of school held by some parents and other adults is sufficient to deter their participation in schools.

However, recent surveys of parental opinion reveal that parents feel able to become more actively involved in their children's education and development. Schools appear to have become increasingly willing to utilise the parents' goodwill. As stated earlier, it is widely recognised that family attitudes and circumstances, and their consequences in terms of parental expectation, support and involvement in their children's schooling, remain the most powerful influence upon children's motivation and eventual achievement.

This is certainly borne out by the highly influential research carried out by the Community Education Development Centre entitled *Raising Standards* which examined parental involvement programmes and the language performance of children in some Coventry schools. The research found that 'the educational benefits of involving parents are very obvious, and have been clearly demonstrated' (Widlake and Macleod, 1984, p.48) and concluded that 'when their parents were encouraged to help, children from less privileged backgrounds were not "doomed to fail" but did as well as, and often better than, their middle class peers'.

It is a notable feature of all studies, across all phases, that good home–school relations always appear as an essential ingredient of an effective school. In some ways, home–school links are essential to achieving one of the National Curriculum's intentions of raising standards. The encouragement these links can give to children in disadvantaged areas – and indeed in all areas – contributes to bringing about an improvement in attainment.

Having good home–school links means that a school:

- **communicates** basic information to parents effectively, and ensures that they have opportunities to see, hear and discuss matters that relate both to their own children and families and to the whole school
- is **accessible,** offering opportunities for parents to visit teachers in schools thereby bringing teachers and parents into regular contact and allowing for discussion about positive developments and concerns
- **can make the best use of parental influence** by identifying and encouraging ways in which parents can support their children
- **promotes greater understanding** of both school and home.

There are a range of approaches to home–school links. Primary schools initiate links with parents before a child starts school. Teachers from a primary school will visit preschool playgroups and nurseries in order to meet parents and their children. Home visits are arranged before a child commences school. Such visits always involve the school writing to parents asking if they can visit and when it would be convenient. Some schools give children preschool gifts of crayons, reading books, name templates or sticky coloured paper – not as a bribe, but as a gesture to welcome the child to the school.

Once pupils are in school, some schools organise an annual home visit by the class teacher. This strategy is functional as well as symbolic. First, parents might be more comfortable talking about their child in their own home than in the classroom; second, it increases the chances of seeing all parents. However, it must remain a voluntary arrangement and parents must retain the right to refuse a home visit.

Home visiting might also take place when a child begins a particular phase or a new school. However, there is overwhelming evidence that links between school and home begin to be less systematic once a pupil enters secondary education. Regular home visiting is virtually non-existent in secondary schools, and few have developed parental involvement policies. The absence of such policies is not an unreasonable omission. Schools find pupils of this age resistant to involving their parents; in fact, some pupils actively discourage their parents from becoming involved.

Once pupils are at secondary school they are capable of coping with the familiar issues of school life. As parents rarely escort pupils to and from school they consequently have little direct contact with school.

To overcome this pupil resistance to parental involvement, managers in secondary schools have to adopt creative and imaginative strategies. These might include:

- curriculum workshops
- social events for parents of new pupils
- involving parents in undertaking practical tasks around the school or its grounds
- involving parents as leaders of sports or special interest groups
- family events or fun activities.

Opportunities exist for involving parents in secondary schools especially where schools have an active adult education, sport or arts programme. Parents can be given particular encouragement to become involved in these activities. In cases where teachers from the school participate in, or are involved in leading, these after-school activities, opportunities are created for parents and teachers to meet more informally.

Managers of schools, regardless of phase, will recognise the significance of parents in their children's education. Home–school links help schools overcome the negative attitudes sometimes held by parents about schools. They promote greater empathy and insight into the community which a school serves and also contribute towards better pupil performance.

Activity 5.2   Partnership: what is it? (R, T)

This activity helps to encourage those working in schools to consider the extent and range of their work with parents, and what they mean by the word 'partnership'. The aim of the activity is therefore to extend understanding about partnership.

1   Complete the sentence 'The aim of partnership with parents is...' in four different ways. Do not think of the practice or activities that comprise partnership work, but look behind this to the principles (for example, 'to value the support given to the pupil by their home' ; or 'to enable teachers and parents to see more of the pupil's all round abilities and development').
2   Write down how categories or dimensions of partnership can be grouped together. Any connections between groups can be illustrated with arrows or line.
3   Consider the partnership 'model' that has emerged and reflect on, or explain, how this has been reached.

Adults in schools

According to Professor Eric Midwinter (1973):

> The community school is one that welcomes in and ventures out. In a visionary future, the ideal consummation would be a situation in which lines between school and community grow blurred.

One of the ways in which schools involved in their community have blurred the lines has been to encourage adults into schools. This participation by adults has taken a variety of forms. It has included the following:

- **Adults reading with children.** Adults come into the classroom and listen or read to children. At some primary schools there exists family reading sessions which include such initiatives as a quarter of an hour at the start of every day being devoted to family reading. Parents accompany their children into the classroom and sit and read together. The child reads a book, comic or magazine, the parent their own book, newspaper or periodical. Each classroom has a selection of books for adults to read and in addition, there might be a community reading area. This community approach to reading is aimed at encouraging parents to read and offer a role model for children.

- **Adults helping in the classroom.** This is a relatively common occurrence in the primary sector. Parents are invited in as an 'extra pair of hands' and generally carry out jobs following directions from the class teacher.
- **Adults as students.** Adults studying in school during the daytime is still quite rare. Some secondary schools do have adults studying in Years 11, 12 and 13 alongside pupils, but adult student numbers can generally be counted on the fingers of two hands. There are schools such as Whitby Community College where an active policy of recruiting adults to the classroom has been pursued. However, among the factors which have restricted adult access to daytime participation are the timetable, the absence of pre-study counselling and lack of childcare.
- **Adults on vocational training courses.** This is becoming an increasingly regular feature of secondary community schools. The funding arrangements introduced by the Further and Higher Education Act 1992 has led to the introduction of a range of vocational courses in schools during the daytime as well as the evening. The courses are targeted at groups such as women wishing to return to work and unemployed people who want to retrain for a new career.

  Schools throughout the country are providing vocational courses. The size of their programmes vary, but some have taken the opportunity to develop a wide range of courses for the community. Schools such as King Edwards (Morpeth), Northallerton College, Bowling Community College (Bradford), and Bodmin Community College are among many schools which have used FEFC resources to effectively promote community-based vocational training opportunities. These courses are normally exclusively for adults, although because the courses are on school premises it does promote the concept of schools being a meeting point for the generations.
- **Adults as a curriculum resource.** This has long been a feature of school life. Most commonly it is found where a member of the community is encouraged to come into school and talk about their job, or their memories. Adults are sometimes asked to demonstrate a special or disappearing skill or trade. In addition, schools encourage adults to help with sports teams or provide additional coaching skills. Where activity sessions are being organised outside of the school day, adults are being encouraged to work alongside teachers during these sessions as volunteers. These out-of-school activities cover a wide range of pursuits including crafts, sport, drama, cookery and the arts.

  Adults are also enlisted by schools to share their skills with pupils. In recognition of the important and valuable contribution adult volunteers can make to development of this community dimension of schools, Education Extra, an organisation established to promote activity clubs outside the school day has encouraged schools to make use of adult volunteers in these clubs

These are examples of how adults have participated in the mainstream of schools. They are not the only ways in which this can happen. If schools are to consider becoming integrated community schools, the barriers that separate the generations must be removed. The above are just a few illustrations of how adult involvement in schools has contributed towards dismantling the 'barriers'.

The community and the National Curriculum

When the National Curriculum was initially prepared there was some concern that the community involvement in the school curriculum would disappear. It appeared to be prescriptive, dictating not only levels of attainment, but also the content of lessons. However, even before the recent National Curriculum Review it was becoming evident that the community could be involved in its delivery.

Before the National Curriculum, schools were making use of community resources in the curriculum. This often meant community service work, or visitors to school who talked about their skills, their experiences or their personal knowledge of a particular place or subject.

Community educators initially thought that the National Curriculum was placing a constraint on this type of learning opportunity. It was suggested that the pressures imposed by the workload generated by the ten foundation subjects meant that community-based activities could no longer be included. Whether this fear was ever completely justifiable is difficult to determine, although the Dearing Review of the National Curriculum and the commitment to the community dimension demonstrated by headteachers and teachers has meant that there is a general acceptance that the subject orders provided plenty of opportunity for the community dimension to be developed. The concept of the 'community-active' National Curriculum has now gradually begun to emerge and is leading to a threading of the community dimension throughout the curriculum. When scrutinising the National Curriculum programmes of study it is, in fact, difficult to see how certain of them could be implemented *without* involving the community.

Gradually schools and their teachers have begun to explore strategies that incorporate local people, local facilities, local issues, local history and geography and local literature into the implementation of programmes of study. This is taking time. Teachers have had to develop competence and confidence to deliver the National Curriculum. They have had little time to examine the necessary strategies to implement a community approach. However, as they have become familiar with the National Curriculum teachers have begun to consider ways of teaching it that makes it more relevant and, indeed, exciting. In schools committed to their community, one of the ways under consideration has been making use of local resources.

A community-active approach to the National Curriculum means community involvement through:

- using community resources and expertise
- sharing the community's facilities and expertise
- arranging visits to local places of interest
- work experience
- involving parents in the delivery of the curriculum
- involving other members of the community in the curriculum
- building links with local industry and businesses.

The school's curriculum is enhanced by these experiences and activities. Managers will wish to ensure that the school's values determine how the school approaches the National Curriculum. However, managers of schools involved in their community will wish to draw part of the content of the curriculum from the community in which the pupils live and use this content to achieve National Curriculum targets. Furthermore, they will wish to see the National Curriculum as an element within the process of lifelong education. Such an approach is endorsed by the preamble to the National Curriculum in the 1988 Education Reform Act where it speaks of the curriculum preparing pupils for adult life.

Management strategies for implementing the community dimension of the National Curriculum will have to include:

1 Exploration with school staff about the reasons for involving the community. Among the reasons will be:

   – It motivates and enhances children learning by starting with the known and familiar.
   – It values the knowledge and experience pupils bring to school.
   – The close proximity of the community makes it a valuable yet affordable resource.
   – By using familiar material parents are more likely to be interested in and supportive to their children's education.

2 A curriculum audit in order to discover and identify the degree to which the community is already involved in the National Curriculum.

3 Identification of areas for involving the community in the curriculum. Managers may look for volunteers among school staff who are willing to

champion community involvement in their subject area, or an implementation team might be established to formulate plans for developing the community dimension.
4   Organisation of professional development that allows teachers to explore the community dimension of the curriculum and to consider ways for developing its introduction into the various subject areas.

Thorns School and Community College in Dudley is one of the schools that has examined community involvement in the National Curriculum. Staff there have designed INSET activities and exercises to promote the development of the community dimension. Schools in Newham in London and some in Devon have also been continuing to use the community in the curriculum with particular emphasis upon involving parents, local organisations and the business community. Their experience of a community-based approach has included the technology, music and physical education aspects of the National Curriculum.

Activity 5.3   Out and about (R, T)

This activity is designed to contribute to managers' considerations regarding involving the community in the National Curriculum. It can be used for personal reflection or as part of in-service training.

The community is a valuable resource for planning the progression of work for specific programmes of study in the National Curriculum. However, to make the most of the community, managers and school staff need to be aware of what is available.

By looking at a local map, the *Yellow Pages*, local 'What's on?' publication, lists of amenities and by drawing on the knowledge of staff and school managers it is possible to gain a clearer idea of how the community can contribute to the delivery of the National Curriculum.

Consider the National Curriculum programmes of study and list the resources that the school could involve from the community in meeting the various programmes of study.

Developing lifelong learners

There is a widespread acknowledgement that education and learning do not end when a pupil leaves school. Lifelong learning is an unavoidable fact, but its benefits are not always consciously understood. Community schools implicitly assume a responsibility for the education of the community, of which pupils of statutory school age form an important element. Community schools should not only be interested in lifelong learning but also lifelong *learners.* Community schools must try to cultivate pupils who consciously wish to continue learning throughout their lives. This will not require them to take out life membership of the local adult education centre, but it does require them to accept the value of learning and the range of sources that can contribute to learning.

Learning throughout life cannot be seen simply as a luxury or irrelevant distraction. Social and economic change means that most, if not all, contemporary education has built-in obsolescence. Even if someone can get a job when they leave school, they can no longer automatically expect to remain in the same job for the rest of their working lives. Change is rapid and continuous. Flexibility and a positive disposition to re-education and retraining will need to be core attitudes if people are to cope. In *The Age of Unreason*, Charles Handy says that 'whatever they may say, neither the young applicant nor the employer today believes that the appointment is forever', and he goes on to say that 'discontinuous change and new professionalism have combined to spell the end of the corporate career for all but a few. Education in those circumstances becomes an investment' (Handy, 1989, pp.126–7).

The challenge facing school managers is to create an environment which is conducive to promoting lifelong learners. Most pupils find schooling enjoyable, pleasant and stimulating. A few find it threatening, alienating and irrelevant. Success, however, is too closely rationed, and this undoubtedly adversely affects pupils' perception of education.

There are some factors influencing pupils' attitude to education that are beyond management's control. The examination system dictates that there will be the successful and the less successful. The nature of society means that, arguably, some families are more able to provide a supportive atmosphere at home than others. The economic climate leads to some families having lower incomes, lower expectations and fewer career opportunities than others.

External factors of this kind are beyond the influence of school managers, but community schools should attempt to modify such negative factors wherever possible. This might include:

- establishing a sensitive and effective pastoral system
- identifying strategies for raising pupil self-esteem
- providing guidance on courses of study pupils may choose to pursue
- celebrating non-academic successes and achievements
- creating a positive and supportive environment.

There are numerous examples of people who did not find school a totally beneficial experience yet went on to return to education or training courses later in their lives. However, today's pupils have to be prepared for conditions of constant change. Conscious efforts must be put into promoting a constructive and positive attitude to lifelong learning as this will inevitably prove an invaluable asset.

Encouraging cross-phase links

Community education is said to represent education's 'seamless robe' – that is, a process extending from the cradle to grave (or as it has been described in the USA as 'tinkle to wrinkle'). The community education ideal is based upon the erosion of barriers to educational opportunity and the removal of obstacles that could prevent the flow from one educational context to another.

Community schools will wish to implement policies aimed at supporting pupils and student progression.

Preschool to primary school

Many nursery and primary schools arrange for parents and children to visit the school before a child is due to start. These visits are used to explain to parents how the school approaches the curriculum and discuss the importance of the parents' role in their children's education. Good preschool provision plays a crucial role in the development of children's education, and teachers recognise the importance of building upon the experiences children have had in preschool learning situations. This is one of the reasons why many teachers in nursery and primary schools want to secure good links between preschool and schools.

Primary school to secondary school

Most secondary schools now have teachers responsible for liaison with primary schools. This liaison includes:

- visiting primary schools to talk to pupils about the school and the opportunities it offers
- organising pupil visits to the school to see the facilities and familiarise themselves with the surroundings
- arranging parents' evenings to explain the work of the school and the opportunities provided for pupils
- organising short courses for primary pupils to attend at the school – examples include computing and swimming courses
- meeting staff of the primary school to discuss parental perceptions and pupil needs.

Counselling for adults returning to school

Schools are increasingly encouraging access to adults. The majority, however, do not provide counselling and guidance to adult returners. Adults are expected to identify their own needs and courses to meet these needs. Managers should consider counselling services to adults returning to pursue courses in their schools. This counselling should include information on:

- the range of provision the school makes available to adult students
- the arrangements for guidance
- the threshold, reception and ongoing support arrangements
- internal signposting
- car parking
- social facilities for adult students
- opportunities for the introduction of teachers and adult students
- access for adults to staff once they have started the course.

It may also be necessary to make counselling available on an outreach basis as some potential adult students will prefer to be met and contacted in surroundings with which they are familiar. Some adults will not have the confidence to return to school, so arrangements will need to be made to develop contact with adults off the school site.

Progression

Although progression does not strictly fit within the concept of cross-phase links, pupils and adult students alike are interested in progression from one educational level to another. For pupils, progression might mean:

- higher education
- further education
- employment
- training.

Adults may interpret progression in similar terms, but may also include the transfer from non-vocational adult education to a vocational course.

Both pupils and adults will have similar requirements in terms of progression. They will want:

- information on options and procedures
- guidance on what will be expected of them on a particular course and as to whether they will be able to cope with the standards required
- details about the cost of the course

- personal support and reassurance
- the opportunity to discuss specific questions
- details of other people's experience
- ideas about where their chosen option might lead.

Community schools will want to encourage progression so that people can achieve their potential. Regardless of age or status, the changes that accompany progression can be unnerving. The move from that which is familiar, comfortable and secure to new environments can be threatening as well as exciting. Managers of schools involved in their community will want to make sure that unnecessary anxiety is kept to a minimum and that the experience encourages personal development.

Partnerships with business

Schools have long had links with their local businesses, and partnerships with business have become increasingly important. The relationship between community schools and the business community has the potential for being mutually highly beneficial.

It is possible for both primary and secondary community schools to develop strategies for working with local businesses. Some of these are discussed below.

Childcare for working parents of school-age children

The Department for Education and Employment (formerly the Department of Employment and the Department for Education) has been encouraging schools to consider out-of-school care. This encouragement was initially supported by funding from the Department of Employment which was channelled through local Training and Enterprise Councils. The charity, Kids Club Network (KCN), played a central role in the implementation of the out-of-school care initiative and continue to be a valuable source of advice. Separate from KCN is Education Extra which campaigns for, and advises on, use of schools for after-school clubs and holiday playschemes. Provision of this type makes available an important source of childcare for working parents and supports local employers' recruitment and retention policies. There are examples of businesses directly funding childcare facilities, either in terms of making a contribution to capital costs or occasionally to revenue expenditure. In these cases, the businesses generally require the identification of a number of the childcare places being reserved for their employees.

Training childminders

People with children below school age and people who live in remote rural areas may still have childcare requirements, but find difficulty in travelling to and from out-of-school care clubs. Community schools can make a contribution by providing training courses for childminders. There are well over 2000 childminders working in the UK yet there appears to be an unsatisfied demand for this service. Trained childminders can provide a secure, reliable and professional childcare provision which can assist businesses to recruit and retrain employees.

Day nurseries

There are a number of examples of day nurseries being provided in community schools, some of which have staff who are fully employed and paid by the school itself. There are other nurseries which schools have created but have been established as legal entities in their own right. There are also nurseries which are independent businesses which hire facilities from the school. Business involvement in these day nurseries is variable. One community school has received a grant from a local business to help it carry out the capital work to convert former teaching areas into a day nursery. In return the business required the option of two permanent places in the nursery for children of its employees.

Day nurseries require qualified staff; they have extended hours of opening and must be inspected by the Social Services Department. However, they do provide an important childcare facility for working parents.

Business and the curriculum

School–business links operate in primary and secondary schools and assume a variety of forms. They can include visits to offices, factories or departments of large organisations. Alternatively, employees from local businesses may visit schools to talk about their work.

Schools are using their links with companies to support the delivery of different subjects in the National Curriculum and, increasingly, General National Vocational Qualifications (GNVQs). There are numerous examples of businesses that provide opportunities for pupils to pursue these studies in the workplace. Companies do provide locations for a variety of activities and simulation exercises based upon their work. This approach to the curriculum includes all subjects and the areas of studies being developed as GNVQs.

Work experience

Every pupil in the final year of compulsory schooling must do a minimum of one week's work experience. This involves a pupil undertaking the tasks and duties of a regular employee, but with emphasis upon the educational nature of the experience. The precise organisation of work experience differs between schools. However, it does provide pupils with the opportunity to sample the world of work and for schools to build links with a large number of local employers. Community schools will not only be interested in the benefits to the pupils, but also in the potential for promoting closer relations with another important element of the local community, namely business.

Further potential links between schools and business

Customised courses for company employees

A number of schools have established facilities for business training. These provide locations for tailor-made courses for local businesses in a range of subjects including IT and languages. These facilities allow employers to upgrade or retrain their employees at a local and affordable venue.

Vocational training according to local labour market trends

This is particularly valuable in areas of the country where there is substantial local economic change and where traditional industries are declining rapidly and new ones emerging. Community schools are providing vocational training aimed at equipping people to work in the emerging industries. This is happening, for example, in former mining and steel-producing areas, with training being supported by funding from the European Union.

Use of school premises by businesses

Schools have a range of facilities that can be used by businesses for sports and social events. Local businesses may use sports halls for their employees' badminton club or for training a soccer team. If the community school has a bar, it may also choose to use the school for social events. In certain community schools businesses have used school halls and other facilities for exhibitions and trade shows.

As in so many areas, being a community school enhances opportunities and scope for development. Community schools need to think imaginatively and laterally. The school–business link can be a two way transaction which can be strengthened if schools give careful consideration to those benefits that they can bring to the partnership.

Activity 5.4   Understanding the barriers to community involvement (R, D, T)

For some adults, school did not represent the happiest days of their lives; they may not have been successful and may not have positive memories of school. Therefore, schools sometimes have to proactively overcome the barriers. The barriers are not insurmountable, but strategies to overcome resistance will require careful consideration.

This activity asks you to try to imagine what it might be like for some members of the community to approach and be involved in learning in a school. How they might feel? What concerns might they have? What things might discourage their involvement?

List the factors that might prove barriers to involvement. Follow this up by identifying ways in which these barriers might be overcome, and what needs to be done to remove the problems the community might encounter when they want to become involved.

6 The management plan and budget management

Critical path analysis

It was George Bush, the former President of the United States, who coined the phrase the 'vision thing' and, for those contemplating the process of implementing community education in their school, it has already been suggested that this is not a bad place to start.

The governors and the senior management team might want to brainstorm a few ideas or carry out some visionary thinking about what community education ought to look like in their school. A good starting point might be to imagine that you have the ability to travel through time and to ask what might be encountered in your school in terms of community education, say, four or more years from now.

This kind of 'fortune-telling' or visioning, can result in the creation of imaginative and exciting perspectives for the future. It can also produce exaggerated, implausible and even bizarre ideas, but, before such ideas are rejected, it is worth examining them from several perspectives. Sometimes the most ridiculous of ideas can sometimes hold the seed of a realistic development.

Some ideas for the future will be extensions of current activities while others will be shaped by an anticipation of external requirements, expectations and opportunities. The visioning approach can make a useful contribution to initial thinking, but it is important to remember that real planning falls into three broad categories: short-term, medium-term and long-term. Managers will have to consider all three categories. The more longer-term the plans, the less likely they will accurately predict the challenges, barriers and opportunities that might be encountered. Conversely, the more immediate the plans the greater the certainty managers will have of the issues that need to be taken into account.

Schools wishing to develop the community dimension will have different planning priorities according to their circumstances. A 'greenfield-site' school – one which does not have a tradition of community education – will want to concentrate on its introduction. A school with a more established community dimension will be concerned with organisational maintenance as well as forward planning.

In either case critical path analysis is crucial. The school that is at an early stage of developing a conscious community education approach may decide, for instance, that its first priority is to establish a parent and toddler group. A longer-established school may wish to ensure its provision for parents and toddlers is strengthened.

In both cases, targets or outcomes have to be established. Managers need to minimise ambiguity of purpose and must be clear about what they want to achieve. In the case of the parent and toddler group the goal may be to 'establish, by the end of the spring term, a parent and toddler group that meets once a week and that attracts 10 parents and their children to each session'. This outcome has to be tackled within a timeframe. If the club has to be up and running by the end of the spring term the lead-in times will have to be identified. Central to critical path analysis are decisions about deadlines and priorities. Planning takes time. The scale of the desired outcome will significantly influence the amount of time required. When a school in Lancashire decided to organise a major exhibition around the wartime experiences of the young Jewish diarist Anne Franks, planning and organisational arrangements were sufficiently complicated and involved that the period from initiation to implementation took slightly over a year. Planners must consider the time each step will require on the way to achieving any agreed outcome.

Once a deadline date has been set for the outcome, a timetable detailing by when different tasks related to that outcome have to be completed must be introduced. Tasks towards the achievement of an agreed outcome are linked; therefore, if one task is not completed by a set date other tasks will be delayed or, in some cases, become impossible to implement. Critical path analysis is best understood in terms of starting from the end of a project at some set time in the future and working backwards through time to the present. This process allows for the setting of milestones which denote when tasks should be completed if schedules are to be maintained. Furthermore, this analysis permits for decisions to be made about not only when tasks have to be completed, but also by whom. Integral to critical path analysis are review meetings. These are meetings set up to monitor progress and timetabled at the beginning of the planning process. In this way, those responsible for completing a task know exactly when they will be required to report progress.

Critical path analysis sits easily within a wider planning approach because organisational management or budget plans contain a number of 'sub-plans' each achieved through following a particular critical path.

Managers must, however, remember that effective planning depends upon their ability to keep colleagues to task. Once outcomes are agreed they must be achieved and this will depend on a number of factors including:

- a realistic timescale
- commitment to achieving the outcomes
- degree of ownership of the outcomes
- extent of participation in the formulation of the plan by those implementing it
- clarity of tasks
- level of communication between those implementing the plan
- resources available to implement the plan
- pressure to achieve other more important outcomes
- experience of implementing earlier plans.

A further, and crucially important, influence on planning and achieving outcomes is the model provided by leadership. The old phrase 'it's not what you say, it's what you do that counts' should be an adage etched in the minds of all managers. Colleagues are more likely to do as managers do rather than as they say. They will not only be watching the 'big picture' but also the subtle, less obvious management actions.

In the context of schools involved with their community this is a major consideration. If the legitimacy of a community education approach rests, to a degree at least, upon participation, then it will be assumed that managers will adopt a participative style. Warning stories regarding the dangers of community participation abound, and managers will therefore wish to steer a prudent course between the extremes of doing everything themselves and letting the community do everything. Managers of community schools will want to involve the community in decision-making and implementation, but they will also have to consider the boundaries of responsibility. The difficulty with this concept of participation is that there can be no set formula.

The approach to transforming leadership in Tom Peters's and Robert Waterman's *In Search of Excellence* (1982), referred to earlier, is based upon legitimate or traditional leaders fostering the leadership skills of others – in other words, leaders encouraging leaders. Among the factors that will affect management decisions about the extent to which this approach is applicable in their situation will be:

- confidence and experience
- the community's level of previous experience of participation
- the nature of the decisions and tasks which have to be undertaken.

Some managers may be tempted to exclude the community from decision-making and the execution of all tasks – an approach which can easily be justified in terms of efficiency, speed, accountability, knowledge or legal constraints. Nevertheless, although participative approaches to decision-making and the implementation of tasks do take longer, the development which takes place within those involved, especially if their participation ends in success, can be extremely rewarding. Schools involved in their community cannot afford to neglect the wealth of opportunities and resources that lie in their locality. There will be various groups and individuals who wish to participate in delivering community activities and schools should examine the potential among these groups. These groups will include:

- parents
- local residents
- representatives of user groups
- local businesses
- adult students
- clubs and societies
- representatives of other local agencies.

Activity 6.1   Community participation in schools (R, D)

It is generally understood that most people act in a responsible way but, despite this, managers are sometimes reluctant to promote extensive participation. They feel people are not ready to take management responsibility. However, according to management guru Tom Peters, for scores of people who have been granted opportunities to participate the results are positive. This activity encourages managers to consider the issue of participation.

1   List the benefits of a participative approach.
2   List the challenges of a participative approach.
3   Write down the name of an organisation that involves participation in its management.
4   Could this organisation be described as successful? If so, why? If not, why not?
5   Who might be involved in participating in the management of the community school?

    - Senior management?
    - Heads of departments?
    - All school staff?
    - Local councillors?
    - LEA officers?
    - Adult tutors?
    - Youth workers?

– Parents?
– Governors?
– Local businesspeople?
– Headteachers from other schools?
– Heads of other statutory organisations in the locality?
– Representatives of community-based organisations?
– Local residents?
– School users?
– Caretakers?
– Administrative staff?
– Pupils?

6   Now identify the most important participants, ranking them in the order 1–10.

Preparing a community education business plan

Until recently, the concept of business planning was not one with which many managers in schools were familiar. Business planning was usually accepted as being associated with commerce and industry. Furthermore, it conjured up images of large sums of money and major financial under-takings. However, contemporary community education in schools no longer assumes this perspective. A business plan of some description has become indispensable regardless as to whether a school is an LEA-designated community school or a self-designated one, or whether it is a primary or a secondary community school.

Local Management of Schools (LMS) has given all schools direct control of their own budgets. Although there may be some variation from one year to another, as a result of changes in pupil numbers or the value of individual pupil units, once the school's LMS budget is set at the beginning of each year it is largely stable and predictable throughout the year. Conversely, the community education budget contains considerable potential for variation. LEA-designated community schools may receive a base budget to cover certain costs. Nowadays, that budget rarely covers all the school's community education costs and, therefore, even schools in receipt of such a budget need to generate additional income. Self-designated community schools will not receive a base budget from the LEA and will consequently have to generate all their community education-related expenditure.

In either case a plan will be required, and this plan will divide into a number of sections. The overall purpose of assembling such a plan is to provide a 'route map' to direct a community school to its preconceived destination. However, it should not be so prescriptive that it fails to allow for taking opportunities that could not be predicted when the plan was prepared. The business plan helps to decide:

- what the school wants to do
- how it wants to do it
- how much will it cost
- how it can be financed.

The business plan will enable a school to set out its community education plans and will assist in determining whether the plans are realistic. To achieve this, school management needs to carefully think through a number of key questions.

What is the nature of the service the school is providing?

This does not require an elaborate philosophical answer, but a clear and concise response as to what service(s) the school is providing. This will inevitably be related to the school's value statement since the service(s) it offers is the translation of these values into practice. A useful rule of thumb is that management should be able to clearly describe the service(s) they provide in about 25 words or even less.

What services does the school's community education programme actually provide?

This question is designed to help the school audit its current range of provision. It requires management to thoroughly examine its present activities. This will not only reveal details of the school's current activities but also whether its programme is consistent with its values. Sometimes schools can be convinced that they are living up to their values, but scrutiny of the programme reveals a gap between reality and rhetoric. The audit will also clarify the type of work the school is undertaking. Due to management's closeness to day-to-day operation it can lose sight of the precise range and direction of its programme. This type of auditing affords the opportunity to stand back from the school's community education programme and realistically assess its content.

Who provides the community education programme income?

This question also requires careful thought as the user or participant in the school's community education programme is not always the person who pays. For example, although members of a yoga club may pay to attend, the school may actually receive lettings income from the club organiser, not the course members. By examining from where income is derived a school can gain a clear perspective as to where to direct its marketing energies. A primary school may discover that most of its users are parents, but that their direct contribution to the school's income is relatively small. On examining income generation they may find that a social services grant supports the parents' usage. Consequently, if the school wishes to extend parental access it needs to encourage greater support from social services. Listing all the sources of the school's community education income and the amounts they contributed during the previous year will prove helpful to the management planning process.

From where does the school obtain resources for community education?

Arguably, the principal question arising from the business plan is 'Will we be able to resource the activities we need to undertake in order to achieve our objectives?' Answering this question will require the school to consider a 'resource analysis' – a process which shows whether present and planned performance are compatible. If a school plans to do more in its future community education programme than it is currently undertaking it has to find out whether it has the resources available to 'bridge the resource gap'. The resources can be categorised into four main areas:

Time

Does the school have the time in terms of people and availability of facilities? LEA-designated community schools often have specific community education staff to carry out community education tasks and duties. In self-designated and primary community schools staff either have to be released from the school timetable, or community education has to be woven into their normal job description. In North Yorkshire's community colleges they have a member of staff designated to community education duties, while in most self-designated schools a member of staff has to be released from the timetable for a certain percentage of time each week.

Time to use facilities is also important. While this generally takes place outside the school day, some schools have found some time during the day for community education activities.

Physical

Buildings, plant, equipment, materials, supplies, natural resources – that is, land and grassfields – all form the school's physical resources. Secondary schools are generally in a stronger position when it comes to access to physical facilities, although primary and secondary schools do often have facilities which can be used in the pursuit of the community education business plan.

People

There are both advantages and disadvantages in being an LEA-designated community school. The key advantage is the appointment of designated community education staff. However, this has the disadvantage that it can lead to the situation where he or she is the only member of staff involved in community education. In self-designated schools community education tasks are generally shared more widely. The problem in some community schools is that the fixation on dual use deflects the school away from integrated community education. In far too many cases teaching and non-teaching staff in community schools do not perceive any difference in terms of their own role to that of similar staff in non-community schools. This is due to a number of factors amongst which is management's failure to convey to all the school staff that community education is more than adult education, youth clubs and dual use. People are probably a community school's richest resource and any community education business plan needs to explore ways that this resource can be maximised.

Financial

In terms of the business plan this can be understood in terms of capital and revenue. Capital consists of the school's assets, such as cash held in a deposit account or building society. Revenue represents income from day-to-day operations of the community school from all sources, and the extent to which it exceeds costs or expenditure determines profitability.

When preparing the business plan try to think in an innovative manner. By approaching the plan creatively it may be possible to overcome certain restrictions or weaknesses. For example, when the school is considering its cleaning contract it might be possible to plan the cleaning schedule in a way that allows for weekend use or twilight activities. Imaginative thinking about the use of existing resources may result in the creation of new opportunities without incurring additional expenditure.

Who are the school's target customers and are they also the funders?

Community schools find that there can be a difference between those who finance their activities and those who use their services. Customers or users may be young people from the local area but the funders could be the

Education Department, the local district council or even the parish council. Sometimes users pay for their own activities, so they are both customer and funder. In analysing who are the customers and who are the funders school management will be able to identify to whom they should direct their funding requests or promotional material to attract resources for their business plans.

Who are the community school's competitors?

Within a school's area of benefit there will be other organisations and providers offering community education-type activities. In some cases there will be direct competition from nearby community schools or further education colleges. However, it is more likely that competition will come from an organisation offering only a small range of similar activities. For example, a village hall might offer keep-fit or craft courses that might compete with the school for participants. Identifying a community school's competitors might require the school to break down its activities into categories such as:

- youth work
- adult education
- sport
- vocational training
- childcare.

Once this has been done, data should be obtained on other competitors. This should include the following:

- location
- time
- frequency
- cost
- organisational arrangements – that is, enrolment; childcare facilities; access for disabled; nature of accommodation used.

The most effective ways of collecting this data is through researching the local neighbourhood and by obtaining information from more official sources including:

- the local education authority
- the local leisure services department
- the library
- the Council for Voluntary Service
- the Citizens' Advice Bureau.

This information will permit management to decide whether provision made by others is sufficiently similar to constitute a duplication of provision or of such a standard that it makes it difficult for the school to compete. In certain circumstances it may be deemed wiser not to compete and it will be consequently agreed not to make alternative provision.

What are the trends and forecasts?

The business plan has to take account of current and developing circumstances. These will be influenced by local, national and European factors. The needs assessment carried out by the school should reveal local trends while information gathered from newspapers, journals and other media sources should provide indicators of developments further afield. Changes in government legislation or funding arrangements can be noted so that the school can begin to make plans for developments that will necessarily follow.

What are the school's community educational priorities?

At this point, the school should be able to list its priorities in the form of a detailed programme for the forthcoming year. The priorities will take account of:

● the current community education programme
● changes in government legislation
● the requirements of funders – for example, the FEFC
● the LEA policy and Service Level Agreements
● needs revealed in the community profile or needs assessment exercise
● other visible or expressed developments
● strengths or expertise available within the school.

How can the school identify income and expenditure?

If the business plan is to be useful it must be framed in financial terms, taking due regard of projected income and expenditure. It is dangerous to identify priorities, establish the programme make an assessment of costs of that programme and, in the light of that expenditure, set income targets. Management has to start from the opposite end. Income has to be projected and then a decision must be made about the level of expenditure that can be afforded. If management planning is expenditure-led grave difficulties will be encountered in establishing realistic income targets. Sources of income and funding are examined further in Chapter 7.

Finance is becoming a crucial consideration for community education, and linking finance to the school's community education provision is an essential aspect of any business plan. A central part of this process is your business planning procedure.

Estimating income

It is easy to make the mistake of establishing overambitious income targets. The most reliable guide to setting income targets is to use the previous year's income as a baseline figure and add a small percentage for growth, but it is unrealistic to think in terms of much more than 3–4 per cent. A school may be aware that its previous year's income is not a reliable guide because of either a known reduction, such as cuts in the budget it receives from the LEA, or alternatively, it may foresee a substantial increase in income as a result of a new source of funding or a one-off grant. A more reliable way of projecting income is to break down the community education programme and prepare a sub-budget or financial report for each area of activity. This will indicate which activities were profitable or the degree of loss a particular activity is incurring.

When managers list or categorise their sources of income they may find that the list is quite extensive and include:

- hire of sports hall
- fees from vocational adult education
- income from the local education authority
- membership subscriptions from youth clubs, senior citizen's groups and so forth
- hire of premises charges.

Primary school income is likely to be more modest and include:

- hire of hall and classrooms
- income from parent and toddler's group
- money raised from a community fete.

For purposes of financial management and planning income it may be useful to introduce the following categories:

- **Guaranteed income.** This is income that is secured and might include income from the LEA or membership subscriptions.
- **Strongly indicated income.** This is income that, judging by available information or well established income patterns, is almost certain to be secured. This might include income, say, from FEFC or from an annual arts festival.

- **Projected or forecast income.** This is income which could possibly be generated but lacks advanced strategies for obtaining it. Examples might be income from an application to the Lottery or a sponsorship arrangement with a private company. This category of income should be prudently estimated. Income cannot be counted until the invoice has been sent!

Estimated expenditure

Some expenditure is relatively easy to predict – for example, staff costs which are usually fixed at a set rate for a given period of time. Other estimated costs are more problematic. Premises-related costs, for example, are notoriously difficult to estimate. Assessing the costs associated with heating or lighting an area of the school during the evening can also be difficult. Schools with bars or refreshment facilities may find it hard to calculate sales and ordering over a twelve-month period.

Expenditure can often be best calculated with reference to previous years. Because expenditure patterns often remain largely constant, details of previous years' costs can be used to inform the forward expenditure planning.

Managers should break down expenditure into various sections and spread projected expenditure into 12 monthly columns. Expenditure headings might include:

- full-time staff salaries
- part-time staff salaries
- tutors' salaries
- youth workers' salaries
- equipment
- fixtures and fittings
- postage
- stationery
- photocopying.

Each organisation will have to develop its own systems of financial management. In many cases the LEA will, or could, provide advice and guidance on management systems. Alternatively, such advice can be obtained from an independent financial source, such as a governor or a parent skilled in these matters.

After the business plan

A business plan is a developmental process in itself. Once it is assembled it will have to be monitored and regularly reviewed and even occasionally rewritten. The school's community education business plan should aim to dovetail into the aims of the whole school. Its preparation should be in keeping with the direction of whole school's development, and changes in the school's direction should be reflected in that of community education. The business plan should cover a three-year period:

- **Year one**: a detailed plan with agreed aims for each area of activity
- **Year two**: general aims for each area of activity
- **Year three**: possible ideas for activity.

A plan review should take place each year, consisting of an assessment and analysis of past performance. Each year outline plans should be brought forward for review and an extra year's plans added.

To maximise the effectiveness of the business plan each of its aspects should have an action plan. Planning will prove to be the key factor in ensuring that ideas are translated into action. It can be time-consuming and, initially, an unfamiliar activity, but it forms an invaluable part of managing community education in schools.

7 Paying the bills

Resource-generation in community schools

It is generally agreed that three of the principal elements of management responsibility are:

- policy direction
- personnel matters and
- resources.

This chapter concentrates on the latter of these three, for without resources it is difficult to develop and sustain community education in schools. Community school managers therefore have to be able to obtain resources and ensure that they are used effectively and efficiently.

The most important issue for managers of community schools is income generation. There are several reasons why this is the case, among which are:

1   The level of support from LEAs for community education has reduced in real terms.
2   Those schools which have adopted a community school policy without LEA designation often do not receive LEA funding.
3   The demands from the community are outstripping current levels of resources.
4   Funding to support innovatory activities often has to be attracted.

The key guiding points underpinning the funding of community education in schools are as follows:

- LEAs will still be a significant source of funding community education even if their contribution is likely to continue reducing in real terms.

- Money is the most important and flexible resource, but there is more to resources than cash.
- Resource generation will have to form a principal element of the work of community education staff.
- Community schools are increasingly becoming responsible for their own community education policy, programmes and resourcing.
- A partnership approach lies at the heart of successful resourcing policy for community education.

The challenges arising from the future funding arrangements for community education can be dealt with successfully, but community education personnel will have to approach resourcing with imagination, knowledge about funding sources and creativity.

Local authority approaches to funding

Over the past few years local authority expenditure has been reduced. However, local authorities continue to show a strong interest in supporting community education and, despite their budgetary problems, will remain a crucial element of resourcing community education in schools. Although predicting the future is a tricky task, it seems that, in the next few years, funding for community education at local government level will derive from a number of departments.

In many **county and metropolitan areas** the LEA will remain the principal funder of community education in schools. However, there are already some variations to this traditional model. Authorities such as Rochdale in the North West, which has a long-established record for community schools, has established a generic department combining leisure and community education services.

The **more recently established unitary authorities** in England and Wales did not have an established LEA and, consequently, some have chosen to establish new departments to support community education in schools. For example, in Hampshire, which has an excellent reputation for its community schools, certain unitary authorities have taken over responsibilities for some of the county's community schools. These unitary authorities have not necessarily located community schools in the new education department and have adopted different approaches to deciding which department should manage and resource community schools. Furthermore, some of the new authorities have decided to introduce different funding approaches to community schools.

Local management of schools

The 1988 Education Reform Act introduced Local Management of Schools (LMS) the centrepiece of which was that schools were given delegated budgets calculated according to an agreed formula driven by pupil numbers. The legislation specified that delegated budgets could only be used for the delivery of the National Curriculum and other specified pupil-related matters. Where school accommodation was used by the community the school had to be reimbursed at cost at the very least. It was outside the law to use the delegated budget to fund or subsidise community use.

This created the need for change as a great many school premises were used by the local authority for adult education, youth work, clubs and associations and local authority-affiliated community groups.

Local authorities responded to this situation by distinguishing between those costs in their budgets associated with community education from those of schools. This process of disaggregation allowed LEAs to identify a budget which they could use to reimburse schools for the community use of premises outside the school day.

However, nothing prevents schools which adopt a community approach to the National Curriculum utilising delegated budgets to involve the community in the delivery of the curriculum and supporting children's learning. A number of local authorities have chosen to extend the concept of a funding formula to delegating budgets for community education, although this is not a widespread practice and most LEAs continue to allocate resources on a historical basis.

The evidence suggests that there is not a standard and accepted form of LEA funding for community schools. Variations even occur within authorities. However, a typology of funding can be represented as:

- discrete
- inclusive
- central.

Discrete funding

This type of funding is generally found in those local authorities where community education councils, trusts or associations have been established based on schools. These are a separate entity from the school, although they usually include school management and staff on their management bodies. The local authority allocates resources to the council/trust/association on the basis of a contract or Service Level Agreement (SLA) and the council/trust/association administrate the programme and employ the staff.

Inclusive funding

In this case, the organisation of community education is seen as the function of a section or department of the school. The school receives a community education budget from the local authority based on a contract or SLA agreed with the school governing body. The SLA states that the school will provide a specified level of community education activities. The school has responsibility for administering the programme and recruiting staff.

Central funding

Here, the school hosts the community education provision which is managed and administered by the local authority. The school is reimbursed by the local authority for premises-related costs. The school's responsibility is to ensure that the facilities are accessible and in an appropriate condition.

Schools without LEA funding

Some LEAs have policies that encourage the designation of schools as community schools but lack the resources to provide ongoing funding. In this situation the only funding a school might receive from the local authority is a start-up grant or a small capital grant.

An emerging trend is self-designation as a community school. This designation is generally inspired and approved by the school governors. It rarely attracts LEA resources and, even if a self-designated school does host LEA adult education or youth work, management responsibility for this provision will not necessarily be transferred to the school. Funding for self-designated schools generally is drawn from a variety of sources, some of which are identified later in this chapter.

Some grant-maintained schools which were designated while they were within the local authority might find that they no longer have access to LEA resources for community education. They, like self-designated grant-maintained community schools, have to identify and seek resources from elsewhere.

Primary schools pursuing a community education approach often find that those aspects they are addressing (parent education, toddler groups and so on) fall outside the scope of LEA funding, but sometimes can be directly related to the National Curriculum. Where this is the case they can fund the activities from the Actual Schools Budget. Alternatively, if they cannot be directly linked to the National Curriculum, resources for these kinds of activities can sometimes be attracted from other sources.

Resource-generation policy

Community education has been incredibly successful in attracting and maintaining resources. This success is even greater when it is considered in the context of the scale of cuts in public expenditure and that community education is not a statutory provision.

However, despite the capability of those managing community education to retain support and use resources effectively, all community schools are having to find ways of seeking additional funding. Managers must adopt a planned and systematic approach to income generation which will include:

- determining core business – that is, determining the school's community education purpose and its client groups
- identifying the key expectations the community places on the school and which of these the school has the resources to meet
- identifying the costs which the school incurs in providing community education
- determining the sources of the school's current income.

Central to this book has been the concept of community education **values** and these will have an implicit influence on a school's resources policy in addition to guiding community school practice. For example, if a school accepts provision for disadvantaged groups as important it will have to seek resources to allow it to work in this sector of the community. Alternatively, if it places importance on sports and recreation this too will influence its resourcing policy. As stated earlier, a values statement spells out for the school, its staff and its community the reason or purpose for being a community school and indicates the nature of the product or service the school is providing. This has to be reflected in the community school's actual community education programme. Resources are essential if schools are to provide this programme.

Step 1

Step 1 of the school's resource-generating policy is to refer to its values statement.

The term 'resource analysis' has already been used in this book. Resource analysis is aimed at revealing any gap which exists between the cost of what an organisation wishes to do and the resources it actually has at its disposal. Organisations have to calculate whether it is realistic, as well as possible, to generate the resources necessary to bridge that gap. Community schools are faced with a similar dilemma. They will know what the community expects them to provide but they will rarely have the resources to achieve all targets demanded by the community.

Step 2

The second step of the resource-generating policy is to detail the programme that a school wants to provide and the levels of funding this will require.

A key dimension of a resource-generation policy has to be an analysis of costs. Precise information about costs is essential for any community school. Local authorities will be able to give guidance, information and data on costs.

The exact information that management of community schools will require will depend on the type and level of activity. However, most will need to identify the cost of the following.

Full-time staff involved in delivering community education

Schools will need to examine salary costs (including on-costs: National Insurance, superannuation and sometimes other employer pension contributions) and the actual time involved in community education to calculate a true estimate of expenditure.

Part-time staff, such as adult education tutors, youth workers and sports technicians

This should be a fairly straightforward process of listing hourly or sessional rates of pay.

Administrative/secretarial staff, including secretaries, clerks and receptionists

Schools will have to decide on salaries or hourly rates of pay and the amount of time which these staff should dedicate to community education duties. Their costs will have to be apportioned across the school's community education activities according to how much time they dedicate to each activity.

Management time

This is the time that managers, other than designated community education staff, devote to community education management tasks. This will involve monitoring the amount of time which management dedicates to community education and a review of the cost of time taken up by other staff involved in managing community education.

Caretaking/building supervision

This can be relatively easy to identify. Schools can do this by examining time-sheets or reconciling the caretaker's letting fee with the level of activities, apportioning a caretaker's charge to every activity that involves a letting fee.

Cleaning

This should include the additional costs to the school incurred through evening, weekend and holiday lettings. Some schools are including this in their cleaning contract specification, but costs have to be allocated to activities and built into their hire charges.

Use of premises

Use of premises costs involve calculating the additional costs associated with heating and lighting – a notoriously difficult calculation. The local authority will be able to give guidance and data, and help may also be available from the gas and electricity companies. Local authorities have adopted various approaches to calculating these premises-related costs, but usually base their calculations on the average cost of heating and lighting the premises, taking such factors into account as:

- seasons of the year
- levels of concessionary lets
- special factors relating to construction of building or heating systems.

The cost should be apportioned across the school's community education programme. An example of an authority's approach to devising a method for apportioning energy costs to a large extensively-used community secondary school is as follows:

> *Actual energy expenditure*: £60 000
> *School use*: 800 pupils × 7.5 hours per day × 5 days = 30 000 school hours per week
> *Community use*: 4000 visitors per week × 3 hours per week = 12 000 community visitor hours per week
> Apportionment of £60 000
> School = 71.5% = £42 900
> Community = 28.5% = £17 100

Administrative costs

These include telephones, postage, stationery and photocopying. Arriving at exact figures can be difficult if community education is not discretely organised. Schools which have community education sections generally have separate billing for administrative services; those which do not operate such an arrangement will have to devise either a monitoring system or a formula for reimbursement.

Replacement of equipment

Certain pieces of consumable equipment – for example, sports equipment, paint brushes or tools used in adult education and youth activities – will have to be replaced more regularly in a community school. The costs associated with replacement will have to be recorded and apportioned across the relevant community education activities.

Maintenance

Additional community use of facilities will entail quicker depreciation of fixtures and fittings. These costs should be included in the school's calculations.

Rentals

Schools will have to identify the additional cost that community education incurs in terms of telephone rentals, fax and television licences. Where facilities for school and community education are separate, costs should be easy to identify but, if the facilities are integrated, costs will either have to be monitored or an agreed formula for reimbursement will have to be devised.

Insurance

Community education will necessitate additional insurance cover. Advice on this should be available from the local authority or a specialist broker. Among the types of insurance policies required will be:

- premises insurance
- content cover
- public liability
- employer liability
- fidelity and fraud
- loss of income
- personal effects
- legal expenses or conflict of interest
- private transport.

Wear and tear

Schools will have to take into consideration the cost of replacing equipment, furniture and fittings since community usage will lead to an increased level of wear and tear. The following example has been recommended by one LEA to calculate the percentage of wear and tear on relevant equipment.

Cost of replacing equipment, furniture and fittings
  used by the community = £x.
Estimated life of equipment = y
Effective depreciation rate £x/y = D per annum
Number of pupils using equipment = N
Number of hours of use by pupils = H
Number of community using equipment = C
Number of hours of community use = U
Increase in wear and tear from community use = $\dfrac{C \times U}{N \times H} \times \dfrac{100}{1} = I$

Additional depreciation required = £ $(D \times I) = A$

Step 3

Step 3 of the school's resource-generating policy is to identify your costs.

Once these have been identified, the school will have information on total annual costs and, following more detailed analysis, the costs associated with each activity. The availability of detailed financial information is important. It will provide an overall picture of how much an activity costs and contributes to determining whether an activity is value for money, or whether the costs of an activity can be modified in any way. Detailed financial information will also be important where:

● sponsorship is being sought for an activity, since this enables accurate figures to be proposed to any sponsor who is being approached to cover all or part of an activity's operational costs
● funding needs to be sought from an external source such as a private company, charity or foundation to subsidise an activity – the cost details allow the school to calculate the level of additional support required
● an activity's income is being used to help offset the cost of another activity. This system of internal cross-subsidy is made more effective if the school knows the level of surplus an activity makes available to use elsewhere in the community education programme.

Step 4

The final step of the school's resource-generation policy is to break down costs into line items (different elements of income or expenditure).

Financial information is essential when schools are planning the overall programme and setting salaries, establishing hire charges and assessing levels of course fees.

Resource partners

In the case of many community schools the LEA is likely to be the main resource partner in providing community education. The LEA will allocate resources on the basis of:

- historical precedent
- a formula
- grant application
- bids
- a contract or Service Level Agreement.

LEAs attach to their resource allocation conditions related to:

- salary levels for part-time staff
- scale of fees for adult education courses and conditions for fee remission
- specific level of provision including level of recruitment, amount of particular provision and quality monitoring arrangements
- equal opportunities measured in terms of participation according to gender, ethnicity, age, economic status and disability.

Regardless of the level of support and resources a community school receives from the LEA the school is still likely to need further resource partners.

In Chapter 1 it was stated that interagency collaboration was a key operational principle for community schools. Unfortunately, this has often been more a matter of rhetoric than actual practice. Nevertheless, the need to devise creative and imaginative approaches to resourcing community schools has led to interagency collaboration and the development of a partnership approach assuming an increased level of importance.

The only resource partnership that many community schools seem to have operated in the past has been that between themselves and the LEA. In fact, analysis reveals that resourcing community education in schools has rarely been the exclusive prerogative of the LEA. In many cases, other local authority departments, particularly leisure services, have been actively involved in community education.

Government policy is leading to responsibility for education and training to not only be delegated but also dispersed. Consequently, local authorities are now only one of a number of agencies with responsibility for education and training. This has led to the emergence of a range of new potential partners for schools, including:

- Training and Enterprise Councils
- the Further Education Funding Council (FEFC)
- City and Rural Challenge organisations
- organisations dispensing Single Regeneration Budgets
- health services
- voluntary organisations
- social services departments
- the police
- community development units
- central government departments
- private businesses.

All of these are interested in aspects of community education, and a partnership approach to these organisations can lead to finite physical, financial and human resources being used more effectively and so avoid waste and duplication.

Recognising the benefits of partnership is one thing, the task of actually initiating and maintaining partnership is a different undertaking altogether. Schools will need to adopt a policy which encourages partnership building. They will want to form partnerships with organisations whose values and interests coincide with their own. They will then wish to turn to their community education programme and find out where resourcing from a partnership can benefit their provision.

Activity 7.1   Funding awareness (R, D, T)

One of the most important aspects of obtaining resources is knowing about the range of funders. This activity is designed to 'audit' current levels of awareness and encourage managers to extend their knowledge where applicable.

Following is a series of questions that school managers need be able to answer if they are to be sufficiently well informed about funding the community dimension of schools:

- Can you name the five Lottery Boards?
- Is the school in an area that qualifies for funding under one of the European Union objectives listed below?
- Do you know what the initials SRB stand for?
- Have you heard of the FEFC?
- Do you have a school hire charge policy?
- Do you have links with leisure services department?
- How much money did you generate from lettings last year?
- Do you know the name of your external funding officer in the county or district council?

Sources of funding

Many managers will have experience of raising funds. This section aims to provide guidance about potential sources of funding and how managers should approach funding sources. This is not an exhaustive list, but does give an indication of the range of areas where resources can be found.

The European Union

Funding from Europe can be a complicated business for those with only a passing knowledge of the arrangements. At the risk of oversimplifying the arrangements it is helpful to know that there are two principal funds relevant to community schools, namely the Structural Funds and the Initiatives Funds.

The European Union allocates extremely large amounts of money to the Structural Funds. It has six Objectives for the purposes of distributing them. Accessibility to the Funds within each Objective is partially determined by geographical area.

The principal focus of Structural Funds and Initiatives money is to encourage social and economic regeneration, so the funding is often linked to retraining or other aspects of vocational education. It is difficult for community schools to make a direct application for funding from Europe, but it may be possible to form one aspect of an application submitted by the:

- Training and Enterprise Council
- district council
- county or metropolitan council
- college of further education.

Most district, metropolitan and county councils employ a member of staff to coordinate and prepare their European submissions. Schools should identify the appropriate officer, make contact and explore whether there are opportunities for the school to be involved in making a bid to Europe.

It is important to remember that:

● all European money has to be matched by public money
● the European financial year runs from January to December
● complete payments from Europe can take up to two years from the beginning of the project
● the application procedure is prolonged and involved.

Central government grants

Central government distributes the majority of its funds to local government through a system of support grants linked to council tax and business rates. However, in addition, it does have grants for which statutory and voluntary organisation can make application.

Each government department has different conditions attached to grants, although the government has now drawn a number of its grants and programmes together into the Single Regeneration Budget (SRB). The SRB is being administered by the regional offices of central government departments, but application is usually made through local government economic development departments, Training and Enterprise Councils or a consortium of local government, Training and Enterprise Councils and the business community.

Schools should seek advice on the SRB from the appropriate officer of the authority. In practical terms, when making grants available, the government is aiming to implement its and local government's policy objectives. Guidelines have been prepared on the SRB and there is an emphasis upon a partnership approach with the community. Sam Clarke in his book *The Complete Fundraising Handbook* says that 'Increasing scrutiny and having to negotiate contracts means that considerable effort has to be put into winning government funds' (Clarke, 1993, p. 38). Schools will probably find it difficult to make an individual bid to the SRB, but may benefit from a collaborative approach with at least one other agency. Information on the SRB can be obtained from Integrated Regional Offices (government offices in the regions), the addresses of which can be found at the end of this book.

In addition to government funds allocated through the SRB procedure small grants are also available from other government departments. Details about the range of grants available can be obtained from the following individual departments:

● Energy
● Health

- Trade and Industry
- Heritage
- Education and Employment
- Environment.

Further Education Funding Council (FEFC)

The Further and Higher Education (FHE) Act 1992 made provision for the establishment of the Further Education Funding Council (FEFC). The FEFC is responsible for allocating resources for all vocational further education, including that for adults. The FEFC funds:

- courses leading to vocational qualifications
- courses leading to 'A' and 'AS' levels
- courses leading to GCSEs
- access courses
- basic education
- English as a second language
- proficiency in Welsh.

Community schools cannot apply directly for funding to the FEFC, but they can ask a college of further education to be a sponsoring institution and apply to the FEFC through the college's governing body. The sponsoring body has to take an objective view on the adequacy of provision for the local population. If the sponsoring body agrees that provision is lacking or inadequate in an area it will forward the application to the FEFC. In most cases a suitable sponsoring body will be the nearest college within the FE sector. However, a number of colleges are now operating a national system of franchising courses, and schools may elect to approach one of these colleges.

Contained within the FHE Act was a major government policy objective regarding the extension of vocational education and retraining opportunities. Community schools have discovered enormous demand in their communities for access to qualifications and training. This has resulted in vocational courses assuming considerable importance in schools' community education programmes.

The FEFC funding arrangements relate to recruitment, retention, completion and qualifications. Funding levels are dependent on the provider's performance in these facets of each of their vocational programmes.

In some areas the LEAs coordinate applications to sponsoring bodies. Such coordination is important where there are a number of schools each making an application for a relatively small amount of funding.

Colleges can refuse to forward an application, but it has to offer an explanation for its actions.

Colleges of further education may choose to undertake outreach work and ask schools if they would be prepared to host vocational courses. In these cases the colleges will reimburse schools for premises-related costs.

Training and Enterprise Councils

There are some 82 Training and Enterprise Councils (TECs) covering England and Wales. These are regional employer-led bodies which plan, administer and provide community-based enterprise development programmes. Each TEC is responsible for:

- youth training
- employment training
- enterprise support and development
- work-related further education
- local initiative funds
- education–business partnerships
- development of National Vocational Qualifications.

Schools should obtain a copy of the local TEC's Corporate Plan. This might help the school identify areas for cooperation in meeting community employment or enterprise-related needs. Further information can be obtained from the local TEC information department.

The Sports Council

The objectives of the Sports Council are to foster the knowledge and practice of sport and physical recreation and to encourage the provision of sports facilities. Sport forms a substantial element of many community schools' programmes and, therefore, those who have facilities need to be aware of the support and advice which the Sports Council is able to provide. The Sports Council can provide capital grants and interest-free loans to local voluntary organisations for the provision of local sports facilities. It has a number of regional offices and information can be obtained on the range of support it can provide.

Local authorities

There are various tiers of local government in this country and, despite the current squeeze on their budgets, they are an important source of funding for community education. Their principal responsibilities, besides education, are for social services, recreation, housing, planning and the environment. Many of these departments are likely to make grants and school management should explore these possibilities.

At the lowest tier of local administration are the parish or community councils. In some areas these councils display an active interest in aspects of community education and have been known to make available small grants for revenue and capital expenditure. Town councils also exist in a number of places and these, too, may be involved in supporting work in collaboration with community schools. Southam School in Warwickshire and Holyrood School in Chard have both benefited in different ways from cooperative ventures with their town councils.

At whatever level of local government the grant-giving process can take a number of forms. It can include:

- giving services, advice or support in kind
- giving premises or the letting of premises at a peppercorn rent
- offering matching funds towards a project that is part-funded from elsewhere
- a cash grant.

Health authorities

Health authorities are currently exploring ways of meeting community care requirements. They are also seeking user advice on the methods for responding to community health needs. Schools might wish to discuss with health authorities and health promotion units the potential for collaborative working to achieve NHS targets. In addition to grants, the introduction of a competitive tendering system in the NHS now provides opportunities to negotiate contracts for delivering services.

Trusts and foundations

There are many trusts and foundations in the UK, ranging from large international organisations that distribute millions of pounds to much smaller local trusts that have more modest budgets. Collectively they donate considerable sums of money each year across a range of causes.

Trusts and foundations are established to give money away. They normally have themes or specified areas to which they are prepared to make donations. They are usually more flexible than government and local authorities and are interested in promoting innovative or new approaches. Most trusts and foundations will only give to charities, so if community schools wish to take the opportunity of applying to trusts they will either have to establish an independent charity or encourage one aspect of their provision to convert itself into one. Some trusts will make donations to organisations which are not registered as charities, but school managers will need to obtain information about a trust's policy before spending time preparing an application.

There are certain national organisations that schools ought to be particularly aware of, including the Foundation for Sport and the Arts and Children in Need. Information about organisations such as these can be obtained from the public library or from publications detailing trusts and foundations.

Funding from the National Lottery

The National Lottery makes 30 per cent of its takings available to support good causes. This is divided into five areas, which are:

- the Arts
- sport
- heritage
- the Millennium Fund
- charities.

A number of institutions have been set up to administer the funds and distribute them according to a predetermined criteria which is detailed in application packs. The various Lottery Boards receive an enormous number of applications. Funding from the Lottery generally has to be matched by the potential recipient, according to criteria laid down by the various Boards. Variations in the percentages needed for matched funding can also be influenced by the locality of the applicant. The Sports Board, for instance, can require lower levels of matched funding from organisations serving disadvantaged areas. However, in the case of the National Lotteries Charities Board there is not a requirement for matched funding. Lottery funding is principally available for capital programmes, although there has been some relaxation of this condition in special circumstances by the Sports, the Arts and Heritage Boards, making funding available for capital and revenue.

Contributions from companies

During the recent past companies' acceptance of their community responsibilities has grown, and, as a result, they have become more involved in corporate donations. Their approaches vary. Many large businesses have a community affairs department with personnel appointed to manage their corporate sponsorship. The biggest companies, between them, give more than £10 million each year, but the collective figure for donations made by smaller companies is also enormous.

In addition to cash grants, companies also provide business sponsorship, secondments, gifts or services in kind and donations of physical items.

Schools should examine the opportunities to apply for company support. This will not always take the form of cash, but may include the donation of time, skills or equipment. They should also consider seeking resources from local small businesses as well as from major national and international companies.

Other sources of public funding

In addition to the sources of funding already outlined above, other potential sources of grants include:

- national or regional arts councils
- the Commission for Racial Equality
- the Equal Opportunities Commission
- the Countryside Commission
- the Craft Council
- the Health Education Authority
- the Rural Development Commission.

Other resourcing opportunities

Within every community there are many different organisations which are potential providers of resources, including sports clubs, membership organisations (for example, World Wide Fund for Nature, Friends of the Earth, etc.), interest groups and churches. Schools may wish to investigate the range of organisations in their community and develop strategies for their involvement. They will not always make cash donations, and, where they do, it is likely to be a modest amount, but they may raise money to help the school purchase a particular item of equipment or donate gifts to support the school's activities. Potential candidates include:

- Women's Institutes
- Round Tables
- Rotarians
- scouts and guides
- church groups
- sports clubs
- employees of local businesses including firefighters, police and staff of large stores.

Approaches to fundraising

There are a number of publications available regarding how to prepare an effective funding application or how to bid for resources. However, the nature of a funding application or a request for resources has to be tailored to the circumstances and to the organisation providing the resources.

The European Union

Requests to the European Union will normally require the completion of an application form. The Union issues detailed notes of guidance, and application forms must conform to the criteria set out in the accompanying documentation. There are prescribed conditions and procedures associated with grants from the European Union and application forms have to reflect the commitment to conform to the associated regulations and purpose.

Government departments

Applications to government departments are usually made through the local authority which usually also administers and disperses any such grants issued. Central government department grants are associated with legislation or a policy initiative and are aimed at supporting its implementation locally. There is usually an application form to complete and often rigorous guidelines around the application procedure. Schools applying for grants will be required to demonstrate that their activities comply with the guidelines. Applications will often be vetted against established criteria by officers and appropriate committees of the council.

Local government

Local government support generally comprises money from grants emanating from central government or grants for specific purposes, such as recreation, environmental or youth work. On the whole, these grants are likely to be open to a degree of negotiation and flexibility. However, the central purpose of the grant is rarely negotiable and increasingly has conditions attached. Application forms are usually available, although sometimes it is necessary to make submission by letter.

Companies, trusts and foundations

Applications to such bodies is largely by letter or through the submission of a written proposal. Occasionally, the company or trust may issue an application form. Clarke (1993), in his book on fundraising says that any applications for funding should be:

- well researched
- concise yet complete

- time-limited
- endorsed by a referee or someone who may be known to the funder
- offering matching funds
- specific in terms of resources required.

Preparing a fundraising proposal

As the number of organisations approaching funders for resources is constantly increasing, a proposal needs to be planned carefully. It should begin with a statement of aim. This aim should be illustrated further by a small number of objectives. The proposal should explain the background to the project, why the proposal is being submitted and what the outcomes will be. It should also contain a detailed budget.

In his book *Writing Better Fundraising Applications* (1992), Michael Norton identifies ten steps to success in fundraising:

1 Make sure that information about your organisation and project are always available.
2 Become known in the grant-making world.
3 Prepare ideas for projects carefully.
4 Consider how you are going to attract funds.
5 Write a clear and succinct application.
6 Plan the management of your proposal.
7 Thank the funder whether they give you resources or not.
8 Maintain contact with the funder.
9 Request further support from funders.
10 Be persistent.

Funders usually request clearly prepared proposals which conform with their priorities. Yet, while the precise format of a funding proposal varies, there is a general style that is helpful in their preparation. First, the project or training programme for which funding is required must be identified. Once this has been done, the proposal should follow the steps below:

1 Write the measurable **objectives** of the project or training. It is likely that three or four objectives are quite sufficient.
2 Prepare three or four paragraphs on the **reasons** why the project or training is necessary.
3 Explain in two or three paragraphs the **background** to the project or training programme.
4 Set out the precise and quantifiable **outcomes** that will result from the project or training.
5 Detail, in not more than three or four paragraphs, the **structure** of the project or training programme.

6 Set out the **timetable** for the project or training programme.
7 Itemise the **budget** and how it will be used.
8 Prepare a two-paragraph **summary** of the project or training programme and use this as an introduction to the proposal. Although it will head the proposal, experience suggests that the summary be written last, so that it summarises the project or training programme more accurately.

How can schools add to their income?

Gifts and donations

Organisations, both large and small, may prefer to give gifts rather than cash. Others may only be prepared to make small donations. Evidence suggests that many community schools generate income from a large number of small donors, as opposed to a small number of large grants.

Sponsorship

In certain countries, private sponsorship has been made available to fund adult education courses or specific community-based sports and cultural activities. This is less common in the UK, but private companies, especially those local to a school, may be motivated to provide resources, especially if they can see corporate advantage.

Exclusive use agreement

A community school might come to an exclusive use agreement with a private company, club or training organisation about access to part of its facilities. This agreement may entitle a hirer to have exclusive use of part of its facilities for an evening or weekend, either for a single event or for regular usage. Although such an agreement might restrict access by the wider community if it were too extensive, a carefully managed agreement could create a regular source of income.

Private hire

Community schools often have facilities that are attractive to members of the community for social events. Hiring out such facilities can yield an important source of income. The potential for private hire includes:

- birthday parties
- social functions (weddings, anniversaries)

- meetings and lunches
- exhibitions
- flea markets/antique sales
- car boot sales
- use of the playground for shoppers parking at weekends.

Schools need to look carefully at hire charges which they may have inherited from the LEA as such charges for accommodation often bear no resemblance to real costs. The local authority usually categorise users into various price bands, often established according to political or social, rather than economic, criteria. Full delegation of budgets to schools and the incorporation of colleges has permitted them to retain all income from lettings and to set their own scale of charges. In setting hire charges, account should be taken of staffing, caretaking, cleaning, energy, administration and equipment maintenance/replacement costs. It is sometimes suggested that if any planned programme covers first use (that is, the cost of opening up), then the rest of the income will be profit. Such a hire charge policy may lead to certain groups and individuals being excluded from hiring premises as they cannot afford to pay. A partial solution to this problem of exclusion is through internal cross-subsidy. That is where surplus income from one activity can be used to underwrite the cost of a concessionary let.

Self-supporting activities

These fall into two categories: those provided by the school, but which attract sufficient participants and income to cover their costs; and those where the school acts as a landlord for a private club or group and charges a hire fee to cover costs at least. These can be useful sources of funding, and the latter type can be provided with little administrative support.

Other sources of income

Certain community schools have specialist facilities and every effort should be made to maximise the benefits to be derived from these, including:

- bars
- sports halls
- multi-gyms
- squash courts
- sunbeds
- copying equipment
- reprographic services
- gaming machines

- outside sports pitches and courts.

Some community schools operate a membership system which also has the potential for generating regular annual income.

The A to Z of funding tips

A is for Authorities

Remember that over 90 per cent of community education has been traditionally funded by local authorities. The diminution of resources for community education from this source causes obvious difficulties and requires innovative solutions from community education providers.

B is for Benefits

Community education yields some important financial benefits: it can be a source of steady, if not immense, income. There may be a reduction in vandalism and serious structural damage as a result of regular extended use of a building. Furthermore, by maintaining heating in the building beyond the end of the school day, there may be a need for less energy the following day to heat the building to an acceptable temperature.

C is for Corporate social responsibility

In those organisations that possess them, corporate social responsibility policies reflect a social awareness. The adoption of such a policy by a community education provider in relation to letting and other activities considered socially desirable would have the objective of setting charges for these at concessionary levels. This would make it necessary to obtain subsidies from self-funding or surplus-generating activities.

D is for Delegation

Community education is not an item that LEAs are required to delegate under the 1988 Education Act. However, some LEAs have decided to delegate community education budgets to schools, colleges and other organisations. Where local authorities delegate budgets they are increasingly likely to withdraw from making direct provision. Delegation usually means that responsibility for the day-to-day policy and allocation of resources for community education is likely to rest with the governing bodies of institutions or the management of organisations.

E is for Energy costs

As these costs are often difficult to estimate, schools should contact their local authorities for information on methods for calculating and apportioning energy costs.

F is for Formula funding

Money allocated to schools through the LMS formula cannot be used to fund community education outside the curriculum. Schools which adopt a community approach to the National Curriculum could consider using resources provided through the formula to involve the community in children's learning. This may include drawing upon the teachers' time to plan and arrange for the community to be used as curriculum support, encouraging parents as partners in their children's education, or developing home–school links.

G is for Grants

Grants are available from a variety of sources to support community education. Most grants are short-term or for one-off events. Before applying for a grant it is important to find out what the funding body gives money for and how you apply. A funding application requires careful research, thorough preparation and careful presentation.

H is for Hire charges

Schools can generate a considerable amount of income from hire charges. Hire charges must reflect real costs, although schools may wish to introduce differentiated scales of hire charges that reflect sensitivity to the circumstances of some groups and individuals.

I is for Insurance

Community schools must have appropriate insurance cover, the cost of which should be built into fees and charges. Schools may choose not to purchase insurance cover for all aspects of use and, if so, they must tell the hirer or user so that they can obtain the necessary cover themselves.

J is for Joint-use agreements

Joint-use agreements have been signed between LEAs and either district councils or metropolitan leisure services departments. These agreements differ. Some entail the district councils making a one-off contribution to the capital programme. In other cases, district councils make a substantial and ongoing contribution to capital and revenue costs. Leisure services are important partners in the provision of certain aspects of community education.

The benefits to be gained from partnerships ought to be reflected in the spirit and letter of agreements between school governing bodies and leisure services departments.

K is for 'Knowable' costs

Certain costs are easier to identify than others. For example, while precise energy, wear and tear and ground maintenance costs are difficult to establish, other costs are more easily identified or 'knowable'. Caretaking rates, hourly cleaning costs, and salaries for personnel involved in community education are relatively easy to assess. Data about these is required if planned programmes of use and pricing policies are to be developed. Methods can be devised to reduce some of these costs through allowing the development of plant or local conditions of service, and use of part-time or casual staff.

L is for the Law

Those involved in the provision of community education need to be aware of the central pieces of legislation affecting community education and use of schools and colleges:

- Representation of the Peoples Act 1949
- Local Government Act 1972
- Education (No. 2) Act 1986
- Local Government Act 1987
- Education Reform Act 1988
- Children Act 1989
- Further and Higher Education Act 1992
- Charities Act 1992
- Education Act 1993.

Further information on legislation can generally be obtained from the local authority Chief Executive's Department.

M is for Marginal costs

All costs associated with community education are marginal costs. The marginal unit is the last to be added. The marginal consideration concerns the smallest possible increase or decrease. If provision is already having to be made at the school for premises-related costs, then community use costs are only those additional costs associated with a specific activity or event.

N is for Non-vocational adult education

Responsibility for the non-vocational education of adults remains with the local authority. It will continue providing adult education that is not covered by Schedule 2 of the FHE Act.

O is for 'On-costs'

Calculations of staff salaries and wages should take account of on-costs. Levels of on-costs vary between full-time and part-time posts. It is important to have details of precise figures for expenditure, income tax and National Insurance purposes.

P is for 'Piggy-backing'

Where a building is being used and paid for by a local authority or another major hirer, it may be possible for any accommodation not being occupied to be hired out to other users, either at a surplus or at a reduced rate. This 'piggy-backing' encourages the concentration of users at particular times in order to obtain benefits from economies of scale. Surpluses generated from 'piggy-backing' can be used as subsidies elsewhere.

Q is for Quality

Clearly the quality of community education is a complex issue. Measuring quality is even more difficult. Before quality can be determined, a community education provider will have to decide what its organisational values are and what a quality community education service looks like. If a provider is investing resources in a service, it will wish to obtain the maximum return. Decisions need to be made before activities are provided about what are the characteristics and criteria of quality and how they can be measured. Conformity to these predetermined quality standards should be monitored and reviewed to ensure the best possible value for money.

R is for Review of expenditure and income

Monitoring and controlling expenditure is crucial. A provider has to project how much income is expected to be generated during the forthcoming year. On the basis of this, it will be able to determine how much expenditure it can afford. Community education providers must remember that funding the programme ought to be realistically assessed based upon a thorough and honest evaluation of the probable income, not a pious hope that the possible might somehow materialise. Therefore community schools should:

- set budgets cautiously
- monitor income and costs
- take action on overspend
- distribute any underspend.

S is for Service Level Agreement

Within local authorities the terminology of client/contractor has become common. Local authorities indicate the level of service they expect and invite tenders from those who believe they can provide services to the stipulated standard. The content and type of Service Level Agreements will differ. Some agreements are based on indicators of quality, some on quantity, while most will include reference to special needs and equal opportunities. Local authorities may well issue Service Level Agreements for adult education, youth work, parental involvement projects and so forth. Providers of community education will be required to submit plans of how they intend to fulfil agreements. Most agreements will have a performance element so that contractors can be monitored and payments reduced or agreements withdrawn if performance is of an unacceptable standard. In addition to the LEA, other organisations will also use forms of Service Level Agreements – for example, the FEFC and leisure services departments enter into Service Level Agreements with schools.

T is for Trusts

Trusts can be an important source of income for community schools. There are numerous large and small trusts in the UK. Some trusts specify in great detail what they will support, who they will support and even where they will make available their support. Schools should find out about the different types of trust and the procedures they have adopted for receiving applications.

U is for Unitary authorities

A number of additional unitary authorities have been created as a result of local government review. These authorities will adopt a variety of approaches to funding community education in schools. Some choose to support the community dimension of schools through the LEA, others through leisure services and others have created new departments that are responsible for funding community education.

V is for Vocational education

In the 1992 FHE Act, adult education is divided into vocational and non-vocational education. This Act made the Further Education Funding Council (FEFC) responsible for all vocational education, which means that the FEFC finances all full-time and part-time education for adults leading to qualifications.

Only colleges of further education, sixth-form colleges or designated agencies can make direct application to the FEFC for funds. It is possible for schools to request that governors of colleges make application on their behalf for funds to the FEFC.

W is for Wear and tear

Community use will lead to additional wear and tear. Schools which have promoted community education will recognise that the reduction in the effective life of equipment will be in direct proportion to the number of people using it and that replacement costs therefore need to be taken into consideration when setting fees and charges.

X is for eXtra-curricular activities

There is sometimes confusion about how formula funding can be used. It is generally accepted that formula funds can be used for:

- governors' meetings
- parent–teachers' associations
- parent evenings
- curriculum workshops
- school team games and sports.

Schools have to be reimbursed at cost by the local authority for:

- adult education
- youth work
- affiliated community groups.

Y is for Youth work

Local authorities have a duty to secure an adequate provision of youth work. In most cases they fulfil this duty through their own managed and directly controlled youth service and through grants to voluntary youth organisations. In many cases these youth clubs are accommodated on school sites, either in schools or in separate youth facilities on school campuses.

If youth activities are being accommodated in schools, colleges or voluntary organisation buildings, they have to reimburse the host at cost. One local authority is issuing affiliated youth groups with vouchers which they can use to hire accommodation from schools and colleges. The colleges and schools can then redeem reimbursements from the local authority by returning the vouchers.

Z is for Zzzzzz...

Community educators must be alert to all opportunities to improve community education provision. None of us can afford to doze in today's turbulent and financially tight climate!

8 A smooth operation

Practical implications for community schools

Education legislation of the late 1980s and early 1990s has had far-reaching implications for the management of community education in schools. By its sheer scope, the legislation has either directly or indirectly affected community education. Indeed, many of the changes contained in the legislation have been quite radical.

However, because of its previous experience, community education was better prepared for some of its impact than other parts of the education service. For example, the introduction of local management of schools (LMS) did not have quite the same startling effect on community education as it did on statutory education, mainly because of community school's substantial experience of budget devolution.

Long before LMS, many LEAs – for example in Cambridgeshire, Northumberland and Somerset – had already introduced schemes to devolve community education decision-making to schools. However, despite this measure of pre-LMS devolution, LEAs had remained the key influential partner formulating, coordinating, advising and monitoring community education in schools.

The role of LEAs has been fundamentally changed by the legislation and this has been reflected in terms of its relations with schools and community education.

Nonetheless, an equally significant influence on the LEAs' role in relation to community schools is that which has been brought about by budgetary constraints. Reductions in LEA budgets has made it difficult for them to exercise the same level of influence that was once possible. The partnership between community schools and LEAs is thus being modified as the power to finance is being revised. Community schooling is increasingly becoming an institutional responsibility, with the schools themselves deciding policy, resource allocation and personnel matters. It appears that as self-designation of community schools expands, LEA influence is changing. This has its advantages and disadvantages. The main advantage is that it promotes greater local ownership and local decision-making. The disadvantage is that the supervision which the authorities once offered in terms of allocating resources rationally, acting as regulator on the distribution of provision, and having the right to intervene in cases where needs were being neglected, they now find more difficult to exercise.

The position of community staff

Community schools are increasingly finding that LMS means that, although they continue to receive LEA funding, the level of this funding is less than they formerly could expect. Consequently, income generation has become a key dimension of a school's community education strategy. This income generation provides an important source of support to the development of the community education programme and the employment of appropriate staff.

LEA-supported community schools may retain a community tutor funded by the LEA, but a number of schools have found that the authority can no longer support such a post, and the schools have either had to generate resources from elsewhere to pay the tutor's salary or appoint a member of staff who is part-funded to manage the community education programme.

The level of seniority of staff responsible for community education varies. In Leicestershire, and to some extent in Northumberland, the senior manager for community education is a vice-principal or deputy headteacher. Similar levels of appointment are found in other schools in different parts of the country. This gives community education influence at senior management level and offers the opportunity for community education to have a certain status in the school.

In other schools the senior manager for community education occupies a middle management position, equivalent to head of department. This gives access to a certain degree of authority and sometimes allows access to the senior management team. The community tutor post regularly involves the leadership of a large team of mostly part-time staff. The tutor is expected to liaise with all sections of the local community, local support groups and pupils. Close links and good relations with school staff is also important, as access to specific areas and equipment is less fraught with problems if the teacher is willing to see their work area used by the community at times outside the school day.

Inevitably, all community schools experience some difficulties with the use of teaching areas by the community. There are occasions when an area is left untidy, or equipment is damaged or there is a smell of tobacco smoke.

Community tutors have to deal with these matters, frequently being called upon to act as mediator between the teacher and community education staff. These situations are sometimes easier to resolve where relations between community tutors and school staff are already fundamentally good.

Job descriptions

Devising a job description for staff with community responsibilities has to be left to individual schools, but, among the community staff's responsibilities are:

- maintaining contact with pupils and the curriculum
- working with parents
- providing cover while teachers undertake home-visiting
- supporting curriculum initiatives with the community
- recruiting, appointing and inducting adult tutors and youth workers
- assessing community needs
- planning, administering and managing the community education programme
- developing outreach work
- managing sports and recreation facilities
- organising the adult education programme
- administering hire arrangements
- community budgets
- promoting the community education programme.

Community staff may not be responsible for all of these duties, particularly if they are part-time. However, a mixture of these duties may feature in community tutor's job descriptions.

Further information on terms and conditions that may be applicable to community education staff can be obtained for schoolteacher conditions from the Council of Local Education Authorities, and on further education lecturers and youth and community workers from the Local Government Management Board. An example of a job description for a Community Education Coordinator is set out below.

Job description for Community Education Coordinator

The Coordinator for Community Education is a member of the Senior Management Team which has developed a style of operation which is far from traditional. It is the task of the team to discuss the issues, to shape the objectives, to determine the priorities and make the decisions. The Community Education Coordinator leads this work in the school, but should understand that these tasks will be shared with others in the Senior Management Team regardless of the areas of responsibility that individuals hold. Every effort is made to ensure that working relationships are, and remain, first-class. The Senior Management Team consists of:

- the Headteacher
- the Deputy Headteacher responsible for Staff Professional Development
- the Deputy Headteacher responsible for Curriculum Professional Development
- the Senior Teacher with responsibility for administration and LMS
- the Coordinator for Special Educational Needs
- the Senior Pastoral Coordinator.

This post involves the leadership of a large team of staff from different backgrounds who have responsibility for the wide range of community education activities. The Coordinator regularly liaises with all sections of the local community, local support groups and professional organisations, the teaching and ancillary staff at the school and has to work very closely with parents and their children. The community school operates into the evening and during holidays and, as a consequence, a fair amount of work takes place outside of normal teaching hours.

The Community Education Coordinator will:

- have a commitment to, and an understanding of, the principles of community education
- be honest and exercise integrity
- provide team leadership skills and have the ability to motivate
- have proven experience in coordination, administration and organisation
- have an understanding of the relationship between the curriculum and community education
- have the ability to relate in a positive manner to all sections of the local community.

Detailed job description

a) Relationship of the post within the school structure

1   Is a member of the Senior Management Team.

2 Is responsible for the development and administration of all facilities in out-of-school hours, i.e. evenings, weekends and school holidays, in collaboration with other members of the community team.

3 Relates on a day-by-day basis to the headteacher and staff at the community school and in particular to the deputy headteachers responsible for the curriculum and staff development, and to the head caretaker over the use of the building.

b) Main duties and responsibilities

1 Oversight of the programme of school involvement with the community and the community's involvement in the school.

2 Day-to-day responsibility for the promotion of the community programme and the monitoring, assessment and evaluation of the contributions made by all those involved in the process.

3 Day-to-day supervision of the community team – that is,

  – all adult and youth tutors paid for by the local authority but under the direction of school management
  – any other employees who may be funded from a variety of sources to benefit the community programme, e.g. Relate, Inner Areas etc.
  – all voluntary helpers.

4 Responsibility for ensuring that the opportunities afforded through the community programme are available to all involved, irrespective of race, gender or disability.

5 Day-to-day handling of all financial matters associated with the community programme.

6 Development of community education across the curriculum.

7 In liaison with the deputy headteacher responsible for staff development, the in-service training of staff at the community school to ensure that community education forms an integral part of the curriculum.

Key considerations for staff with community responsibility

The post of coordinator, organiser or supervisor of community education in a school will take a range of shapes and forms.

Some schools may have funds from the LEA to make a full-time or part-time appointment. Other schools will attract resources for a particular project or area of work and will want someone to undertake its management. Alternatively, schools may allocate the role of community education to an existing member of staff and release them from the timetable for an agreed period of time each week.

Regardless of the type and extent of the appointment, schools will need job descriptions. Although they will, however, approach the design of job descriptions differently, there are key considerations:

- What is the purpose of community education in the school and what are the key functions the appointee will need to perform?
- What is the title of the post?
- Will it be full-time or part-time?
- Is there a salary or incremental point associated with the appointment?
- Who will the appointee be responsible to?
- What are the responsibilities and the main tasks the appointee will have to undertake?
- Will the appointee teach in the school – if so how much non-contact time will they have?

Line management

If the member of staff responsible for community education is at deputy head level he or she will be line-managed by the headteacher; if he or she is at head of department level he or she may still be managed by the headteacher, but more likely by the deputy headteacher. Where there is a community education trust, council or association the community tutor will also be accountable to the organisation's management committee. The headteacher and chair of governors may or may not be a member of that committee.

Community tutors often work long and unsociable hours. They are in schools during the evening, weekend and holidays. Conditions for community tutors vary, but commonly they are required to be on-site five evenings in every two weeks.

Some schools have taken steps to either remove or not appoint a discrete post for community education and instead have written a community responsibility into the job description of all senior management. The purpose of this policy was to encourage an integrated approach to community schooling. Despite the advantages to this approach, there are some difficulties including that, if managers regard community education as low-priority work, it can be neglected. Equally, some community education duties are time-consuming and difficult to fit within the framework of the timetable, so these duties may not be fulfilled.

On the other hand, where there is a discrete community education post, the post-holder may be perceived by the majority of school staff as not really 'belonging', and the community tutor can become an outsider lurking on the margins of the community school. This gap can be closed through well formulated values, a positive approach on the part of the headteacher and/or the attitude of the community tutor. Good examples of effective integration of community education staff into the main body of the school exist at South Molton Community School in Devon, Richard Lander School in Truro and Minsthorpe Community School in Wakefield. There are many other schools that have also achieved similar situations.

Management and leadership

The skills required by senior management in relation to community tutors and community education in general are different from those necessary to successfully manage a traditional school. Effective management of community education in schools requires headteachers to:

- initiate and/or own the school's community education values and live these out in their actions
- develop an understanding of community education and examine how it can be applied to their school
- encourage all interested staff, teaching and non-teaching, to have a commitment to community education and, where possible, positively acknowledge and reward staff
- accept that the purpose of community education can sometimes be different from statutory education and consequently may require a different set of expectations and the application of other types of performance criteria
- recognise the importance of promoting a participatory approach to management of community education. This will require a facilitating rather than a directive management style
- set concise, realistic and measurable targets for community education
- encourage community tutors to be imaginative, enterprising and businesslike
- recognise that community staff have different working hours to other school staff, but must account for their hours.

Leadership is a key preoccupation of many writers on management, not least Tom Peters. In *Thriving on Chaos* he writes extensively about leadership and makes a comment that is particularly pertinent to community education managers:

'Empowering' really boils down to 'taking seriously'.... How do we get people to come forth and give answers, to take risks by trying new things bound to fail at times? Near the top of the list is listening – that is, taking people seriously by the act of listening per se, making it clear that you do take people seriously by what you do with what you hear. The most effective leaders ... empower others to act, and grow, in support of a cause that both leaders and followers find worthy. (Peters, 1987, p. 525)

This transforming style of leadership – leaders creating leaders – is at the heart of community education management. It is easier said than done, and much more threatening to the manager than most styles of management, but it is essential if communities are to become involved and the skills that reside within individuals and groups in the community are to be realised.

Activity 8.1   The role of the headteacher (R)

The headteacher is central to the development of the community dimension of any school. He or she has a number of key roles to fulfil. This activity is designed to develop a fuller understanding of the role of the headteacher in the school which wants to promote a community dimension.

Prioritise the following statements in an order of 1–10 (1 being the most important, 10 being the least important).

A headteacher

- ensures appropriate caretaking and cleaning arrangements are agreed
- establishes a management structure and encourages governors to set up a community subcommittee
- liaises with outside agencies
- prepares and provides the school's community values
- manages community staff
- oversees the financial and administrative management of the community dimension
- prepares the school's community policy
- ensures staff develop the community dimension of the curriculum
- appoints the community education teacher/coordinator
- encourages positive attitudes to community among all school staff, whether teaching or non-teaching.

Premises management

This book has attempted to argue that the community dimension of schools goes beyond the concept of community use of premises. However, use of premises is an important element of the community dimension and the management of premises and the associated operational arrangements are a critical consideration. This section explores some of the principal issues associated with the smooth operation of community school facilities.

Caretaking and cleaning

Caretakers are quite literally the gatekeepers of community use of schools. Their function assumes enormous importance, and their attitude to community use has a critical influence upon its effectiveness.

Managers must make sure that caretakers, who will be required to open and secure the building, sometimes at unsociable hours, are involved in the development of the community school. Supportive caretakers are invaluable to the promotion of community involvement. There are endless stories about the highs and lows of the relationship caretakers have with community education which often reflect the impact they can exert on the level and quality of provision.

Caretaking systems vary between community schools. Some schools operate a shift system, some an hourly overtime rate, and some link fees to the number of rooms used.

The attitude of caretakers is a significant factor influencing community use. In LEA-designated community schools, caretakers take the job on the understanding that there would be extensive evening, weekend and holiday use of the building. Where schools are designated by the authority or self-designate with a caretaker already in post, full and open discussions need to be arranged with caretaking staff about the implications for them of working in a community school.

Caretaking can be a crucial factor in influencing whether a school wishes to develop community education. Schools which have good relations with caretaking staff do not wish to adversely affect these by introducing new duties associated with extensive community use. However, most caretakers do not have a negative attitude to community education so long as they are consulted. In fact in some schools, such as Isambard Brunel School in Portsmouth, the caretaker has assumed a key role in the promotion and development of community education.

In schools which have community councils or community education subcommittees the caretaker is sometimes a member. There are considerable benefits flowing from their involvement, including the dissemination of information to caretaking staff and the promotion of a sense of ownership.

To avoid having to call upon the caretaker to open and close each time the school is used, some schools have introduced the idea of named keyholders. These key-holders – often members of the school's cleaning staff – either regularly or occasionally open and lock the building.

Cleaning arrangements also need to be considered when developing community use. Schools are usually cleaned at the end of the school day. Secondary schools have a team of cleaners who are contracted to carry out a range of cleaning duties. In the case of schools used by the community these cleaning duties will have to be supplemented or the hours during which duties are carried out will have to be renegotiated.

Most community schools will want to continue with a main clean at the end of the day, not only to prepare the school for the pupils for the following day, but also to clean areas to be used in the evening and weekend by the community.

It is unlikely that every area of the school will be used by the community outside the school day, but some areas will be subject to heavy usage. Schools will have to consider cleaning these areas in the early morning before the school day commences. Typically these areas will be:

- gymnasiums
- halls
- sports halls
- changing rooms
- entrance halls.

In the case of secondary schools, such revisions to cleaning duties could be included in the contract negotiated with those tendering to provide cleaning services. In primary schools, it will probably be the caretaker or a single cleaner who will have to be approached about undertaking the morning tidy-up and cleaning duties.

Hiring arrangements

Letting premises can prove an important source of revenue for the school and offer access to valuable facilities for the community. To maximise the mutual benefits to school and community, effective systems for hiring premises need to be established. The school has to decide which facilities are to be available for hire and must calculate the costs associated with hiring facilities in order to establish a scale of charges. The school may wish to introduce a differentiated scale of charges which reflects its values or priorities. It may want to categorise hirers and charge, for example, local residents, youth organisations, parents groups, fees that are lower than those it would charge to commercial users or those who are hiring the premises for social events.

Among the factors to be taken into account when fixing hire charges will be:

- the size of the facility
- duration of use
- the category of hirer
- frequency of use
- purpose of use
- numbers of participants

- the nature of the activity
- use after a certain time in the evening.

The hiring policy will have to be written down and made available to members of the community who wish to use the premises and should contain reference to:

- details of insurance
- details of charges
- fire regulations
- condition of facilities after use
- payment schedules – when payment should be made
- notice of cancellation
- deposits and caution money against breakages or damage
- suspension of lettings if facilities are required by the school
- details of furniture or equipment available to hirers.

The local authority may be able to give guidance on drawing up conditions for hirers.

Hire arrangements should take account of any general principles of hire such as:

- a statement to the effect that it is the school's policy to encourage the community use of its premises, especially by those who live within the immediate vicinity of the school.
- an indication as to which facilities are available for use, including the playing fields
- conditions for hire and categories for letting premises which might be:
  - the full charge rate which applies to functions open to the community, but not for educational or not for the exclusive benefit of the immediate community.
  - the concessional charge rate which applies to activities that either are for community educational purposes as defined by the school or for specific identified groups such as youth or senior citizens or residents of the school's immediate community.
  - free of charge concessions which apply to activities related to the school's corporate life – that is, governors' meetings – or with the welfare of pupils – for example, parents' evenings.
- conditions for the use of the school, including use of specialist areas such as kitchens and sports facilities.

Charges will need to take account of:

- caretakers' fees
- cleaning
- energy costs
- size of facility hired
- market rates at other establishments
- wear and tear
- secretarial or staff time to operate booking system
- telephone and postage
- grounds maintenance.

Additional charges should be considered for the hire of furniture, specialist items of equipment, kitchen equipment and changing rooms.

The school will also have to consider operating different types of hire arrangements. Some bookings such as use by adult education courses or sports clubs, will involve long-term or regular use. This can be recorded on a booking form. Casual users of badminton or tennis courts, sunbeds and multi-gyms are likely to want to book at short notice and by telephone.

Most schools have little problem in establishing arrangements for taking bookings for longer term or regular bookings. Difficulties do occur, however, with sessional bookings which are an essential part of casual use. This requires someone to be available for long periods of the day to receive calls, record hirers' details on a booking sheet and have a system for collecting fees from users.

One of the main problems with casual use is that if there is no sufficiently effective system for taking bookings, facilities will not be used to an optimum, thereby denying schools revenue.

Conversely, if all facilities are hired out on a long-term basis it can lead to certain groups and individuals being excluded. Community schools face a major dilemma. Should they block-book facilities and guarantee income or establish a more flexible booking system and risk underutilisation?

There may be an argument for mixing block-bookings with casual use arrangements, but adequate systems must be implemented to respond to casual users. In addition, schools will need to take care not to restrict casual use to those times when no one else wants the facilities. The block-booking system is not without its problems. Schools generally hire out facilities for a term, two terms or the whole year. There is tremendous demand for certain facilities such as halls, sports hall and gymnasiums and this demand is also concentrated on certain times of the week. Schools sometimes find the same club or organisation occupying the same time-slot in the same facility for several years. While this can become a cosy relationship, it also prevents both innovation and access by other users. However, when a school tries to change a longstanding hirer's arrangements it can create genuine problems and tensions. Therefore careful thought should be given to advance block-booking arrangements and to time-banding facilities which are in great demand.

Many schools continue to retain a system by which the sports hall or hall is hired out from 7.00 pm to 9.00 pm. Consideration might be given to restructuring its hire arrangements. For example:

- 6.00 pm–7.00 pm: family groups/youth activities
- 7.00 pm–8.30 pm: clubs and adult courses
- 8.30 pm–10.00 pm: clubs and casual use.

By time-banding in this way the use of the facilities could be maximised and a wider range of needs satisfied.

Office administration

Adequate administrative arrangements must be made to support community education in the school. The functions of administration will depend upon the scope of the community education programme. It may include:

- **Booking school facilities.** Administrative staff may be required to issue and receive booking forms, deal with telephone bookings, record bookings on a booking sheet, inform the caretaker, make sure that requested furniture or equipment is available, organise any school catering which has been requested and send out confirmation letters and invoices.
- **Adult education administration.** Administrative staff may be required to book rooms, ensure that equipment is provided, issue registers, deal with adult education tutors' queries, provide information to students, collect fees, collect tutor's claim forms, liaise with the caretaker and check class sizes.
- **Secretarial duties.** Administrative staff may be required to prepare letters, reports and other appropriate materials, deal with enquiries, send out orders, dispatch invoices and process receipts.
- **Financial work.** Administrative staff may be required to manage petty cash, bank fees and other cash income, maintain ledgers, produce income and expenditure reports, administer salaries for part-time staff, monitor budgets, maintain accurate records, chase up debts and control orders.

The school may choose to appoint a secretary or administrative officer exclusively to deal with community education matters. Alternatively, the duties associated with community education could form an element of a secretary's or number of secretaries' job descriptions.

The administrative implications of becoming a community school have to be understood and either introduced into the job description of existing staff or included in the job description of a designated administrator/secretary for community education.

Reception and signposting

Schools should give careful consideration to their 'threshold' arrangements – that is, the planning, presentation and organisation of the school's entrance and reception facilities.

Despite the fact that schools are public buildings, for some people the school is remote, unwelcoming and inaccessible. Undoubtedly, personal experience and attitudes affect their perception of school, but some of the factors affecting community participation derives from the adequacy or otherwise of signposting and reception arrangements.

Schools are not the easiest of buildings to enter. Main entrances are not always located in the most obvious places. Architectural design, building extension and modernisation and security arrangements adopted by schools might lead the casual observer into thinking that some schools have deliberately attempted to keep the community out. Signposting can help overcome confusion and uncertainty about access to school buildings. Schools with clear and regular signposting arrangements convey positive messages to the outside community that they are welcoming and accessible places. They prevent visitors experiencing embarrassment by trying to gain entry at secured doors or at points of entry well away from reception.

Signposting is required both outside and inside the building. Members of the community will not be familiar with the school's layout and good internal signposting will assist their movement around the premises.

Another important consideration is adequate external lighting. In many cases weekday community use will be during the evenings, and people will be on the school site after dark. Schools will therefore have to give thought to whether footpaths, drives and car parks have sufficient lighting. This is a particularly important consideration if the school wishes to attract women and older people.

Once entry into the school has been negotiated the first point of contact will be reception. Initial impressions can have a significant effect upon members of the community. Receptionists should project the school's values. They should be welcoming, friendly, helpful and efficient. Some members of the community will have found coming into school quite emotionally demanding, and their anxiety ought to be acknowledged and efforts made to help them feel at ease.

The physical construction of reception areas can have an influence on the school's image. Closed doors, officious signs, small reception windows and compact areas can sometimes be off-putting. Desks or counters and brightly lit foyers can project a more open and public image. Nevertheless, the receptionist's attitude can overcome any immediate adverse physical impressions. Those with good interpersonal skills can easily compensate for restricted physical facilities. Conversely, those with less well developed skills can negate the advantages of a first-class reception area.

In *The Pursuit of Excellence* (Peters and Waterman, 1982), Tom Peters introduces the concept of TDC or Thinly Disguised Contempt. He believes that people can easily spot TDC and consider it to be a key influence upon people's attitudes to another person or an organisation. Community schools and their staff must avoid TDC and attempt to ensure that members of the community are dealt with in a sensitive, considerate and decent manner. A useful motto might be 'Treat other people as you yourself would like to be treated'. The receptionist's personal judgement of others should not be reflected in his or her approach to members of the community. Receptionists can be a valuable source of encouragement, and this ability should be supported by school management. In fact, training and supporting reception staff should be a priority if a school is to present a welcoming and positive first impression to its community.

Safety and security

Events have recently taken place, which have challenged the concept of the 'community-friendly' school; a number of recent incidents have drawn attention to safety and security in schools.

Most schools continue to be committed to community access and avoiding the promotion of a 'fortress mentality', but, quite rightly, school managements wish to have procedures in place which minimise the possibility of risk to pupils, staff and community users of their school.

The following actions may be taken by schools to ensure that they remain welcoming and secure:

- Limit the number of entrances to the school, ideally aiming to have only one external entrance where the school has its reception. All other external doors should only be capable of being opened from the inside.
- Have well trained and supported receptionists who can deal with the public in a sensitive way. Well trained and skilled staff are more likely to be able to diffuse a potentially aggressive confrontation.
- Have adequate signposting both outside and inside the building to make it more difficult for people to wander about claiming that they have lost their way.
- Use signing-in procedures and visitors' badges – a procedure accepted

by most people as reasonable. Schools can then monitor visitors for fire and safety purposes and also easily identify people.

● Consider introducing spotlights and surveillance cameras to ensure the security of both the premises and property as well as making sure that people are sufficiently protected.

Marketing and promotion

Definitions of marketing all include reference to meeting and identifying customer needs. The market-oriented community school means adopting a community-focused perspective, making provision of a kind and in a way that matches community needs. If community schools are to use marketing to best effect they need to be clear about who their customers are and develop strategies to address this group. Community schools must also identify community needs and be aware of what resources the school has to meet them.

It is important to understand the marketing mix. The four 'Ps' of marketing are:

● Product
● Price
● Place
● Promotion.

Product is what the community school provides in the way of services. This should relate to the school's values. The product is the interpretation of these values into practice.

Price and place are self-explanatory and refer to the price of the service and its location.

Promotion cannot be done until the school has identified what the customer needs, developed an appropriate product to meet those needs and made it available at a price and in a location which matches customer demand.

Any marketing strategy has to include **market research** – this gives a community school a better understanding of both its customers, and competitors and serves as a foundation for a marketing plan. Market research does not have to be time-consuming, complex or expensive to be useful. A community school can obtain an enormous amount of information by simply asking members of the community, parents and/or users of the school about their needs, likes and dislikes. The purpose of market research is to replace misinformation and assumption by fact. It is a form of needs assessment under another name. Market research or needs assessment will not only help the school identify problems, it will also uncover potential opportunities.

Marketing involves delivering to the community the activities and services they want. A written marketing plan is an integral part of a successful community school. The plan should:

- pinpoint its target market – identify those parts of the community at whom the school should aim its services
- build a competitive edge – encourage members of the community to see its services as valuable and superior to its competitors
- build a marketing strategy around its target market and its services.

Large schools may be able to prepare quite formal marketing plans, while primary schools may choose a less formal approach. In either case, the involvement of as many staff as possible in the planning process is advisable. The marketing plan will result in the community school dealing with three broad questions:

- Where are we now?
- Where are we going?
- How are we going to get there?

The market research should appraise the school of its current situation, allowing it to establish self-achievable objectives which will spell out the destination of its marketing strategy. The strategy it pursues should detail how the community school intends to achieve its marketing objectives.

A further consideration is how to promote the school's activities and services. The promotional strategy must be linked to the other element of marketing – communicating with the market. Promoting the community school's activities involves:

- informing the community what the school is offering
- persuading the community to participate.

Promotional work is easier if the school is offering what the community wants. The difficulty for some community schools is that what the community wants may not be seen by community educators as what they need. If this is the case the school may wish to persuade the community that its interests are best served by pursuing an approach which is different from their expressed desires.

Community schools can promote themselves through advertising. Regular advertising is critical to marketing success. It can:

- inform
- persuade
- remind.

Ways of advertising to potential customers might include:

- sending pupils home with information for parents
- distributing handbills at places where parents congregate
- circulating fliers at parent and toddler groups
- placing handbills in clinics, doctors' surgeries and libraries
- delivering promotional material through people's letterboxes
- producing a locally circulated community newsletter or paper
- including a supplement in parish magazines or local free press
- placing an advert in the local newspaper
- advertising on local radio.

Advertising is not the only form of promotion, however. Other strategies are also available, such as:

- **Community education brochures.** These give details to the community about how the school operates and the range of experiences and opportunities that are available to them. The brochure will emphasise the benefits the community can obtain from participating in the community school's activities.
- **Exhibition or events.** These provide an opportunity to see examples of what the community school can provide and may include 'taster opportunities' where members of the community can try some of the activities the community education programme offers.
- **Press releases or editorial copy.** Producing this type of material can yield considerable promotion for activities without the expenditure associated with advertising. Local newspapers are often short of editorial copy and will welcome information about local events or achievements.
- **Word of mouth.** This is one of the most effective forms of promotion. The best source of promotion is satisfied customers. Community schools should use every opportunity to communicate on a one-to-one basis with members of the community. They should also encourage satisfied customers to tell other members of the community about their experience.

When considering marketing, schools should examine their image. They need to know how they are perceived by the community and whether that perception matches the community's expectations. A school is a school, but if it wants to promote its image as a community school it needs to know:

- what image does it currently project?
- what image does it want to project?

The community school should collect data and information from the community on its current image. It will have to assess how it can bridge the gap between how it is perceived and how it wishes to be perceived. School managers will have to explore the possibilities for closing the gap and the strategies it needs to pursue.

Community schools are generally considered to be characterised by their programmes, use and activities, but in fact they are essentially about attitudes, working practices and ethos. Changes in superficial appearance are relatively easy to achieve, but changes in values and culture are more difficult and take much longer.

Performance indicators and quality control

'Quality' became one of the education buzzwords in the late 1980s. It had already become an increasingly important preoccupation for business and industry as they struggled to respond to market pressures, and quality management had emerged as an important dimension of any modern organisation. Industry and business wanted to secure their part of the market and one of the ways in which they believed this could be achieved was by ensuring quality. A number of textbooks have been written on quality management, and systems have been introduced in an attempt to assess and maintain quality. The essence of quality is that customers get value for money. As Phil Crosby, a quality expert, says in his book *Quality without Tears* (1986), the service or product has to conform to customer requirements.

Education has adopted a similar stance. Customers (pupils and parents) should get value for money for the education they have paid for through their taxes. Education is required to meet customer expectations. A problem arises when a simple comparison is attempted between the service a customer can justifiably expect of a holiday in a hotel with the service a school provides to pupils or the wider community.

OFSTED

In order to monitor and inspect the quality of education, the government introduced legislation in 1992 which led to the establishment of the Office for Standards in Education (OFSTED). The OFSTED arrangements introduced a framework for the inspection of all schools. Every school has to be inspected every four years by a team of OFSTED-trained inspectors led by a registered inspector.

Headteachers, governors and others involved in community schools have always regarded community education as making an important contribution to both the quality of life in the school's community and to the personal, social and academic life of the school's pupils. Consequently, schools which regarded themselves as integrated community schools wanted to be inspected as a whole. They wanted to ensure that attention was paid to all aspects of the school and the contribution of each part to its standards of education, including the effects community education has on pupils' achievement.

OFSTED recognises that the contribution of parents and the wider community can have a significant effect upon pupil performance and has given increased attention to those in the revised framework. Furthermore, the revised framework and the OFSTED framework on the inspection of adult education and youth work contains acknowledgement of the role of integrated community schools.

The OFSTED (1995b) guidance on inspection of secondary schools states that, where community education is part of the school's provision, its inspection should determine how far it serves both the school and its community. The official definition adopted by OFSTED of what constitutes a community school dates from the Education Reform Act 1988:

> a school is a community school if a) activities other than school activities are carried out on its premises b) all non-school activities which are so carried on are carried on under the management or control of the governing body. (s. 47)

OFSTED is clearly interested to know the extent to which schools are drawing upon local experience into the school curriculum and extracurricular activities. Furthermore, they are indicating to inspectors that they should consider how community education links with the aims of the school.

The OFSTED guidance states that evidence is required of observations of community education activities in and out of school, scrutiny of plans and records including surveys and other assessment of need, and inspectors are guided to hold discussions with pupils, staff and users.

The OFSTED arrangements have demonstrated that the quality of service provided by the school has to be evaluated at many levels and arguably on an individual pupil/student basis. The service which schools provide is complex. Conforming to requirements cannot wholly be based upon customer perceptions or articulated requirements. Professional mediation regarding what is required is also important. However, to naively assume that schools know best is a poor starting point for establishing a quality service. Quality can only be achieved through dialogue between schools and their customers.

Managers may believe that they know what the community wants, but without exploring this with members of the community any belief can only be regarded as professional assumption. Consequently, it may not conform to customer requirements and, therefore, will not be regarded by the community as a quality service.

Quality Assurance

It cannot be repeated too often that the essence of quality is rooted in a community school's values. The values contain the school's purpose, and that purpose is converted into practice through the community school's programme and attitudes. Through needs assessment or market research, the school will identify the needs of the community and, so long as resources can be found, the school will aim to meet the community's expectations. Once community needs have been broadly defined, management has to decide how it will implement meeting those needs. This is where quality management becomes significant.

Members of the community will have expectations of all aspects of the school's community education service including:

- publicity
- reception
- advice and guidance
- staff attitudes
- accommodation and equipment
- teaching or instruction
- information
- organisational arrangements
- refreshment facilities.

Management is responsible for ensuring that all aspects of the services to the community are of an appropriate standard. That standard is determined by customer expectations, and those expectations can only be ascertained through listening to the community. Listening might take the form of written evaluations as well as sitting down and having a conversation with a member of the community. Schools will have to devise their own mechanisms for obtaining feedback, but managers do have a duty to listen to the community's expectations from wherever they are derived. Phil Crosby and others place great emphasis upon the role of management to:

- act as a role model for quality
- clearly articulate and demonstrate their definitions of quality.

Crosby (1986) states that his discussions with US companies have revealed that quality is only realised when senior management is dedicated and committed to improvement. Management has to demonstrate its commitment to quality by living it out themselves. Furthermore, staff working in the community school need to agree and codify what is expected of them when undertaking a particular task. It is no use for management to complain that someone has not done a job properly if they were never given information about how to do the job properly in the first place.

> Management really has three basic tasks to perform: establish the requirements that employees are to meet; supply the wherewithal that employees need in order to meet those requirements; spend all its time encouraging and helping employees to meet those requirements. (Crosby, 1986, p. 59)

Some organisations establish massive manuals that break down into intricate detail how specific jobs should be done. It is for each individual school to decide whether it has the time and resources to embark on an exercise of this kind. King Harold School in Waltham Cross found that when it undertook its successful pursuit for the quality 'kite-mark' BS5750, it was required to produce documentation and details relating to all its organisational functions. However, even if a school does not want to pursue a quality kite-mark, they may wish to establish indicators of performance that have been negotiated between the school and its customers.

Performance indicators

Performance indicators contribute towards assessing effectiveness. They are predetermined notions of what it is hoped to achieve – benchmarks determining whether sufficient progress has been made. Performance indicators can be useful in monitoring organisational and personal performance. They are analytical management tools which act as triggers to further investigations or review.

Performance indicators can be used to assess quantitatively and qualitatively so long as criteria for assessment are clearly defined and understood. They should be developed to measure short-term performance outputs, and also demonstrate the contribution to agreed levels of quality.

Good performance indicators should be:

- **Credible:** that is effective, reasonable and appropriate. It is pointless to establish an indicator of performance that is quite obviously impossible to achieve, given the available physical and human resources.
- **Comparable:** so that they are capable of being applied to similar situations or organisations so that a degree of comparison can be drawn and so that they will detect deviation from agreed standards.
- **Reliable:** that is, they should do what they say they will do.
- **Time-limited:** unless this is built into the indicators, its usefulness will be impaired.

- **Easy to establish:** if the introduction of an indicator is difficult and time-consuming it will probably be ignored or only partially implemented.
- **Cheap and easy to collect:** unless the data that indicators require can be identified with relative ease the monitoring will not take place.

The application of performance indicators in schools will vary. A community school may wish to establish indicators for access, lifelong education, interagency collaboration or the curriculum. Establishing too many indicators should be avoided, as they will be difficult to operate and the data obtained from their application will be unmanageable.

For performance indicators to be applied effectively the school first has to define the problem. It might be possible to encapsulate the problem in a question. For example:

'How can we recruit more students to our vocational courses?'

The performance indicator might be:

'Increase participation in vocational courses by 5% over the next six months.'

The performance indicator would be monitored and, regardless of whether participation increased by 5 per cent or not, evidence to explain the situation would be sought. This investigation could lead back to issues of quality, marketing, or even to issues beyond the school's control. Whatever the outcome, though, the performance indicator will give management data which can be used to influence and inform future decisions.

Staff development

'If we want things to stay as they are, things will have to change', says the favoured nephew in Lampedusa's *The Leopard*. Things are changing. Devolution of management has meant that many of the LEAs' functions have moved to schools, including staff development.

Staff development in schools is linked to its development plan. The plan details the direction the school is moving and staff development aims at providing the skills, knowledge and understanding staff need to ensure that the school reaches its destination.

The implications for community schools are that community education should either permeate the school development plan or merit a supplement to it. A necessary prerequisite of a community school is the existence of positive attitudes among the staff towards a community education approach. These attitudes can be promoted through staff development. Community education ought to be central to every school, and staff development can play a crucial role in the achievement of this aim.

Staff development is not just about training, it is also about the enrichment of the employee in school. Attitudes, beliefs and skills are crucial to successful community schools, and staff development should be designed to promote attitudes that are actively supportive or positively sympathetic to the notion of being a community school.

For most teachers, community education is a different approach to that for which they were initially trained. It challenges the notions of who schools work with, what the desired outcomes are and the relationships with the community at large.

It has been said on numerous occasions throughout this book that there is no single universal model for community schools. The starting point for community education in schools is an analysis of their position in terms of:

- relations with the community
- resources
- time
- personnel.

Once a school has agreed, in community education terms, what it stands for – its purpose – it must develop actions, practices, structures and attitudes to reinforce its values. Staff development has a key role in this reinforcement process.

The essential elements of an effective staff development policy are as follows:

- the formulation of a **statement of values**
- the adoption of **practices and actions related to those values**
- **the design of appropriate job descriptions** that refer to being a community school or include community education-related tasks
- reference to being a community school in **the selection and recruitment of staff**

    - advertisements should advise applicants that the school has a community approach, and at each interview, candidates should be asked about their attitude to community education and working in a community school

- acknowledgement of community education as an aspect of **induction**
- **the evaluation of community education** in organisational and staff reviews

- **the inclusion of community education in the school development plan** or the development of a community education supplementary plan
- the provision of **training in community education** for all staff
- **resource allocation** to community education
- **the adoption of structures** which reinforce community education in school.

Staff development should be relevant to the role of each member of staff, so the amount and type will vary accordingly.

Induction has a key role in developing community education. Generally induction is a carefully planned programme for new staff and is usually used to give a new employee the opportunity to learn more about the job, make relationships and meet other people who will be useful in the pursuit of the job.

If a community school is to be developed, both current and new staff will need to go through a form of induction. Clearly, not everyone will be directly involved in community education, but an understanding of the concept of being a community school needs to be understood by *all* staff. This applies equally to teaching and non-teaching staff.

A community school requires staff development and, although this staff development should include training, it should also include opportunities for other forms of personal and organisational development related to community education. A community school's staff development policy should consider strategies for taking community education from the margins of the school and locating it in the mainstream. This means looking at issues such as:

- relations with parents
- links with pupils' homes
- the curriculum
- attitudes to adults in school
- working with other agencies
- working with volunteers
- communication skills
- benefits and challenges of being a community school.

Staff development might include developing awareness of the needs of particular groups as well as issues of access and lifelong education.

All staff – both teaching and non-teaching – should be encouraged to be aware of their role in the development of a community school. Some staff will play a more active role than others. Staff development should contribute towards the nurturing of leadership that is dedicated and committed to the promotion of a community school. Although it is not essential, and not always desirable, to have one person given sole responsibility for community education in school, it is important that some post-holders do have community education as one of their key tasks.

Community education should not be the exclusive responsibility of senior management nor a community tutor. Community schools succeed where the responsibilities for development is assumed by the majority of school staff.

The evidence suggests that schools which develop their community dimension have the potential for not only extending the concept of lifelong education and enhancing pupils' learning, but also for making a crucial contribution to improving the quality of community life. Experience has proved that developing as a community school requires time, organisational commitment, and above all, leadership.

School leadership which chooses to embark on the journey of consciously developing as a community school must remember that it has taken over 70 years for community schooling in this country to reach its present stage. However, with interest in the community dimension continuing to grow among management of schools there is a possibility that, as we move towards the next millennium, Henry Morris's vision, formulated back in Cambridgeshire all those years ago, of all schools being community schools might take a step closer.

References

Austin, N. and Peters, T. (1985), *Passion for Excellence*, New York: Warner Books.

Clarke, S. (1993), *The Complete Fundraising Handbook*, London: Directory of Social Change.

Crosby, P. (1986), *Quality without Tears*, New York: McGraw-Hill.

Drucker, P. (1990), *Managing the Non-profit Organisation*, Oxford: Butterworth-Heinemann.

Handy, C. (1988), *Understanding Voluntary Organisations*, Harmondsworth: Penguin.

Handy, C. (1989), *The Age of Unreason*, London: Arrow Books.

Midwinter, E. (1973), 'The EPA school', *Urban Education*, April.

Nisbet, J. *et al.* (1981), *Towards Community Education*, Aberdeen University Press.

Norton, M. (1992), *Writing Better Fundraising Applications*, London: Directory of Social Change.

OFSTED (1995a), *The OFSTED Handbook: Guidance on the Inspection of Primary Schools*, London: HMSO.

OFSTED (1995b), *The OFSTED Handbook: Guidance on the Inspection of Secondary Schools*, London: HMSO.

Peters, T. (1987), *Thriving on Chaos*, New York: Harper & Row.

Peters, T. and Waterman, R. (1982), *In Search of Excellence*, New York: Harper & Row.

Street, P. (ed.) (1992), *Schools, Governors and Community Education*, Coventry: CEDC.

Widlake, P. and Macleod, F. (1984), *Raising Standards*, Coventry: CEDC.

Further reading

Allen, G. and Martin, I. (1992), *Education and Community*, London: Cassell.
Allen, G. *et al*. (1987), *Community Education: An Agenda for Educational Reform*, Milton Keynes: Open University Press.
Atkinson, R. (1995), *Cities of Pride*, London: Cassell.
Bastiani, J. (1989), *Working with Parents*, London: Routledge.
Bennett, A. (1994), *Writing Home*, London: Faber & Faber.
Braun, D. (1990), *Community Primary Schools*, Coventry: CEDC.
Dadzie, S. (1993), *Working with Black Adult Learners*, Leicester: NIACE.
Department for Education and Employment (1995), *Your School, Our School*, London: HMSO.
Devlin, T. and Knight, B. (1990), *Public Relations and Marketing for Schools*, Harlow: Longman.
Dreyfoos, J. (1994), *Full Service Schools*, New York: Maxwell Macmillan.
Fitzherbert, L. (1995), *A Guide to Major Trusts*, London: Directory of Social Change.
Gelsthorpe, T. (1995), *Managing Community Education*, Leicester: Secondary Heads Association.
Handy, C. (1984), *The Future of Work*, Oxford: Blackwell.
Handy, C. (1994), *The Empty Raincoat*, London: Hutchinson.
Howe, D. and Wilson, J. (1995), *Bringing Learning to Life*, Coventry: CEDC.
Hudson, P. (1993), 'Managing your community building', *Community Matters*.
Hurd, H. (1994), *A Guide to the National Lottery*, London: Directory of Social Change.
Merton, B. (1996), *How Are We Doing? A Guide to Self-review*, Coventry: CEDC.
Munn, P. (1989), *Parents and Schools*, London: Routledge.
Ree, H. (1985), *Educator Extraordinary*, London: Peter Owen.
Reeves, F. *et al*. (1993), 'Community need and further education', *Education Now*.

Street, P. (1991), *Looking at Community Education*, Coventry: AMA/CEDC.
Street, P. (1992), *A Price Worth Paying*, Coventry: CEDC.
Street, P. (1994), *Preparing a Community Education Business Plan*, Coventry: CEDC.
Webster, K. (1992), *Reach Your Community*, Oxford: Oxfordshire County Council.
Whalley, M. (1994), *Learning to be Strong*, London: Hodder & Stoughton.
Whitling, B. (1993), *The Children Act and School*, London: Kogan Page.
Wolfendale, S. (1989), *Parental Involvement*, London: Cassell.

Useful addresses

General

Action for Governor Information and Training
Manor Hall
Sandy Lane
Leamington Spa
Warwickshire CV32 6RD

Tel: 01926 413740

Arts Council
14 Great Peter Street
London SW1P 3NQ

Tel: 0171 333 0100

Basic Skills Agency
7th Floor
Commonwealth House
1–19 New Oxford Street
London WC1A 1NU

Tel: 0171 405 4017

Community Development Foundation
60 Highbury Grove
London N5 2AG

Tel: 0171 226 5373

Community Education Development Centre
Woodway Park
Wigston Road
Coventry CV2 2RH

Tel: 01203 638660

Community Matters
8/9 Upper Street
Islington
London N1 0PQ

Tel: 0171 226 0189

Community Service Volunteers
237 Pentonville Road
London N1 9NJ

Tel: 0171 278 6601

Council for Local Education Authorities
Eaton House
66a Eaton Square
London SW1N 9BH

Tel: 0171 235 1200

Directory of Social Change
Radius Works
Back Lane
London NW3 1HL

Tel: 0171 435 8171

Education Extra
17 Old Ford Road
London E2 9PL

Tel: 0181 983 1061

Forum on the Rights of Elderly People in Education
Bernard Sunley House
60 Pitcairn Road
Mitcham
Surrey CR4 3LL

Tel: 0181 640 5431

Further Education Funding Council
Cheylesmore House
Quinton Road
Coventry CV1 2WT

Tel: 01203 863000

Heritage Lottery Fund
National Heritage Memorial Fund
10 St James's Street
London SW1A 1EF

Tel: 0171 747 2087

Kids Club Network
Bellerive House
3 Muirfield Crescent
London E14 9SZ

Tel: 0171 512 2100

Local Government Management Board
41 Belgrave Square
London SW1X 8NZ

Tel: 0171 235 6081

Millennium Commission
2 Little Smith Street
London SW1P 3DH

Tel: 0171 340 2001

National Council for Voluntary Organisations
Regents Wharf
8 All Saints Street
London N1 9RL

Tel: 0171 713 6161

National Governors Council
Glebe House
Church Street
Crediton
Devon EX17 2AF

Tel: 01363 774377

National Institute for Adult and Continuing Education
21 De Montfort Street
Leicester LE1 7GE

Tel: 0116 255 1451

National Literacy Trust
Swire House
59 Buckingham Gate
London SW1E 6AJ

Tel: 0171 828 2435

National Lottery Arts Board
Arts Council of England
14 Great Peter Street
London SW1P 3NQ

Tel: 0171 312 0123

National Lottery Charities Board
7th Floor, St Vincent House
30 Orange Street
London WC2H 7HH

Tel: 0171 839 5371

National Lottery Sports Board
Lottery Unit
Sports Council
PO Box 649
London WC1H 0QP

Tel: 0171 388 1277

National Youth Agency
17–23 Albion Street
Leicester LE1 6GD

Tel: 0116 247 1200

Pre-School Learning Alliance
69 Kings Cross Road
London WC1X 9LL

Tel: 0171 833 0991

Scottish Community Education Council
West Coates House
90 Haymarket Terrace
Edinburgh EH12 5LQ

Tel: 0131 313 2488

University of the Third Age
c/o BASSAC
13 Stockwell Road
London SW9 9AU

Tel: 0171 737 2541

Workers' Educational Association
Temple House
17 Victoria Park Square
London E2 9PB

Tel: 0181 983 1515

Youth Clubs UK
Keswick House .
Peacock Lane
Leicester LE1 5NY

Tel: 0116 262 9514

Government offices for the regions

East Midlands
The Belgrave Centre
Stanley Place
Talbot Street
Nottingham NG1 5GG

Tel: 0115 971 2759

Eastern
Unit 7
Enterprise House
Chivers Way
Histon
Cambridge CB4 4ZR

Tel: 01223 233385

London
Riverwalk House
157–161 Millbank
London SW1P 4RR

Tel: 0171 217 3456

Merseyside
Graeme House
Derby Square
Liverpool L2 7SU

Tel: 0151 224 6302

North East
Stanegate House
2 Groat Market
Newcastle upon Tyne NE1 1YN

Tel: 0191 201 3300

North West
Sunley Tower
Piccadilly Plaza
Manchester M1 4BE

Tel: 0161 952 4054

South East
First Floor
Bridge House
1 Walnut Tree Close
Guildford GU1 4GA

Tel: 01483 882255

South West
4th Floor
The Pithay
Bristol BS1 2NQ

Tel: 0117 900 1700

West Midlands
6th Floor
77 Paradise Circus
Queensway
Birmingham B1 2DT

Tel: 0121 212 5050

Yorkshire and Humberside
City House
New Station Street
Leeds LS1 4JD

Tel: 0113 280 0600

Sports Council

National Office
16 Upper Woburn Place
London WC1H 0QP

Tel: 0171 388 1277

Regional offices

East Midlands
Grove House
Bridgeford Road
West Bridgeford
Nottingham NG2 6AP

Tel: 0115 982 1887

Eastern
19 The Crescent off Tavistock Street
Bedford MK40 2QP

Tel: 01234 345222

London and South East
Crystal Palace National Sports Centre
PO Box 480
Ledrington Road
London SE19 2BQ

Tel: 0181 778 8600

North West
Astley House
Quay Street
Manchester M3 4AE

Tel: 0161 834 0338

Northern
Aykley Heads
Durham DH1 5UU

Tel: 0191 384 9595

South West
Ashlands House
Ashlands
Crewkerne
Somerset TA18 7LQ

Tel: 01460 73491

Southern
51a Church Street
Caversham
Reading RG4 8AX

Tel: 01734 483311

West Midlands
Metropolitan House
1 Hagley Road
Five Ways
Birmingham B16 8TT

Tel: 0121 454 3808

Yorkshire and Humberside
Coronet House
Queens Street
Leeds LS1 4PW

Tel: 0113 243 6443

Index

COMPETENCE & ACCOUNTABILITY IN EDUCATION

Edited by
Peter McKenzie, Philip Mitchell and Paul Oliver

MONITORING CHANGE IN EDUCATION

In a world of apparently diminishing resources, there have been consistent calls for more effectiveness and efficiency in education, and there can be no question that those involved in education will face calls for increased accountability.

Meanwhile the competence 'movement' has stressed the idea that education and training should be primarily concerned with achieving measurable outcomes, particularly those which have credence in the workplace. Opponents suggest that this is often to the detriment of the knowledge and understanding normally regarded as crucial to competent performance, yet it is likely that this kind of measurement will increasingly become an index of accountability.

The papers presented in this volume examine these concepts in a variety of contexts, ranging from school-based teacher training to the assessment of NVQs, and from recent government legislation to the Smithers Report. A variety of views are expressed, which should be of interest to all those concerned with current trends in education.

1995   168 pages   1 85742 279 1   £25.00

Price subject to change without notification

ENVIRONMENTAL ISSUES IN EDUCATION

Edited by
Gill Harris and Cynthia Blackwell

MONITORING CHANGE IN EDUCATION

Effective environmental education is an essential requirement for a sustainable future, yet it is acknowledged that public understanding of major environmental issues remains poor. This book provides an overview of recent research on the degree of understanding of environmental matters and surveys resources available to support the delivery of environmental education and the development of environmental policies.

The findings of research on attitudes to the environment and on understanding of environmental issues among children and young people in the UK and across Europe are presented, together with a survey of practising teachers' awareness of environmental matters.

The book also examines the link between environmental education and green consumerism, and looks at the contribution which both formal education - in schools, further and higher education - and informal education via the media can make to the development of environmental awareness.

Finally, the book attempts to establish indicators for the evaluation of environmental education programmes, to secure the development of positive attitudes and a genuine, life long responsibility for the environment.

1996   224 pages   1 85742 331 3   £27.50

Price subject to change without notification

PARENTS, EDUCATION & THE STATE

Edited by
Cedric Cullingford

MONITORING CHANGE IN EDUCATION

The role of parents in the education system is crucial and increasingly recognised as being so, not only by teachers, but by parents themselves and politicians. Parents are seen to have an influential part to play in support of schools and are also asked to take a more controlling role.

This book examines the reality of parents' place in the education system: How important is their contribution? What do they think of it? What do teachers and children think of this? What kind of impact do parents have on the academic and social futures of their children? And what do their parents really think about the political changes?

This book brings together original research and distinguished contributors, to deal with important issues. It analyses what is going on based on empirical evidence from parents, children and teachers, and draws out the political implications.

1996   196 pages   1 85742 338 0   £30.00

Price subject to change without notification

Psychology and Education
for
Special Needs
Recent developments and future directions

Edited by Ingrid Lunt, Brahm Norwich
with Ved Varma

The education service is in the process of basic changes in curriculum, organisation and funding. This inevitably affects special needs education which, while adapting and undertaking significant changes, is retaining the progress made since the implementation of the 1981 Education Act. This edited book provides an overview of and commentary on the broad areas of policy and organisational aspects, and curriculum and teaching matters concerning special needs education. Within these pages the reader will find pointers for future developments in the field.

The book is in three sections and shows that special needs education relates to all aspects and levels in the education system:

• Provision for special needs, which includes chapters on early identification, provision for clumsy children, specific learning difficulties and those with communication difficulties.

• Teaching, assessment and support approaches, which includes chapters on school-based developments to meet the needs of children experiencing difficulty in learning, individual strategies for investigation and intervention, and reflection on the role of educational psychologists.

• Policy, organisation and training, which includes chapters on implementing the 1981 Education Act, school clusters, international perspectives, lobbying and teacher education for special needs.

1995   264 pages   1 85742 306 2   £35.00

Price subject to change without notification

Using Museums as an Educational Resource

An introductory handbook for
students and teachers

Graeme K. Talboys

Visits to museums have long been recognised as an important aspect of the education of young people. Not only do they introduce them to the many and varied forms of our material culture, they also introduce them to social, philosophical, and spiritual themes and situations that are difficult to encounter elsewhere.

This book aims, through the discussion of theory and practise, to provide a comprehensive introduction for students, practising teachers, and other educators to all that is required to make good educational use of museums. It does so in a number of ways. To begin with, it explores what a museum is, their value in the education of children, and why they require special teaching skills. It then goes on to look at the practicalities of planning, preparing, and conducting a visit. Next, it introduces the basic skills involved in working with the resource (such as sites, buildings, objects, and the like) that are required to make the best educational use of museums. Finally, it considers ways of following-up work done outside the classroom.

Graeme K. Talboys, who has a degree in philosophy and education as well as a teaching qualification, has considerable experience as a teacher, a community education worker, and a museum education officer.

1996   **208 pages**   **1 85742 344 5**   **£30.00**
Price subject to change without notification

arena

THE
ASSERTIVE TEACHER

GWYNNE WILSON-BROWN
• • • • • • • • • • • • • • • • • • •

"The great merit of this book is that the compilation of case studies of teachers has been carefully chosen." Career Teacher

Gwynne Wilson-Brown believes there is a world where teachers have personal power stemming from high self-esteem and open, honest behaviour. In this self-help book she shows professional teachers how to improve their self-esteem and exercise their personal rights with professional responsibility, demonstrating integrity and dignity.

The skills range from asking for what they want to confronting unpleasantness; from helping another to solve a problem to managing their own feelings. Exercises at the end of each chapter encourage the teacher to try a new way.

The book goes further than merely giving skills. It takes the skills into the real world of the teacher. Case studies show how assertive language makes interactions in schools satisfying and rewarding. Men and women, primary and secondary teachers can pursue their goals through work and maintain good relationships even when needs clash.

This book provides a holistic approach to human interactions in the school, whether they be with children or with authority.

Gwynne Wilson-Brown is an independent Education Consultant specialising in personal and professional skill training for professionals. She has 20 years experience in the classroom, teaching in both primary and secondary schools.

1994   **134 pages**   **1 85742 218 X**   **£15.95**

Price subject to change without notification

50 POPULAR TOPICS

A resources directory for schools

Compiled by David Brown

You are resourcing a topic, and you don't know who publishes what. The school doesn't have all the publishers catalogues you need, and you don't have addresses for those you haven't got.

THE RESOURCES DIRECTORY has been compiled to solve all these problems. The 50 most popular primary and secondary school topics are included with a huge range of books, videos, software, kits, packs, equipment and schemes for all ages between 5 and 13.

Over 2500 items from 50 suppliers are included, together with their addresses, all grouped in topics, cross-referenced in a comprehensive index and with an appendix of schemes in science, technology, geography and history.

David Brown is a schoolteacher with over 20 years teaching experience in primary, middle and secondary schools. He is also author of 'GOLDMINE', published by Arena.

1995   201 pages   1 85742 163 9   £15.00
Price subject to change without notification

arena

The Dictionary of
Educational
Terms

David Blake & Vincent Hanley

Contact ratio, Key Stages, hidden curriculum, opting out – but what does it all mean? If you have ever felt bewildered by the constantly changing language in the school world this is the book for you!

This convenient and easy-to-use book of reference to education in England and Wales brings together information on the National Curriculum, the world of schools, the legal framework of education, key educational ideas and much more. The extensive cross-referencing and comprehensive list of abbreviations and acronyms make it an ideal tool for teachers, governors and parents alike. **The Dictionary of Educational Terms** is an invaluable guide to a complicated field – can you afford to be without it?

David Blake and *Vincent Hanley* are Principal Lecturers in Education at the West Sussex Institute of Higher Education.

1995   203 pages
Hbk   1 85742 256 2   **£30.00**
Pbk   1 85742 257 0   **£14.95**

Prices subject to change without notification